LEEDS GUITAR DICTIONARY

2400 CHORD POSITIONS

By

F. CHIERICI

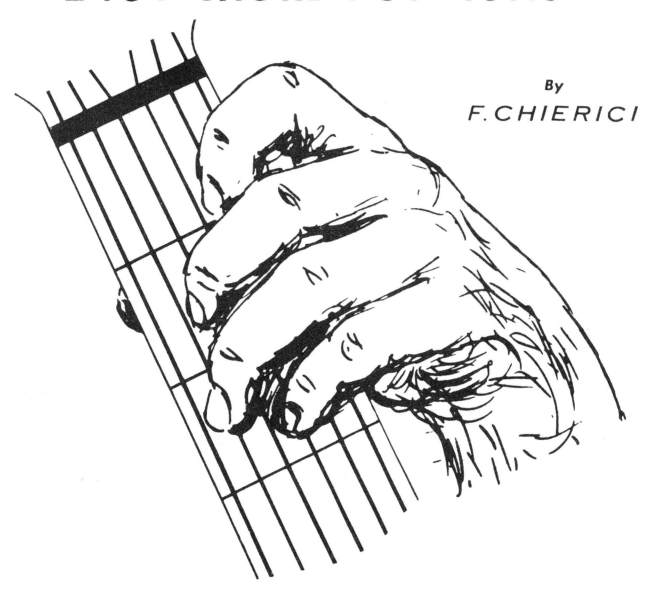

© Copyright MCMLXII by EDIZIONI MUSICALI FARFISA, Ancona, Italy
MCA MUSIC LIMITED, London, England.

Exclusive Distributors:
MUSIC SALES LIMITED
8/9 Frith Street, London W1V 5TZ, England.

INTRODUCTION

After playing and teaching guitar for many years, I have discovered that there is not a book which can quickly give the way to finding a required chord.

My book consists of 2400 positions, which can be found easily and quickly, by means of the index.

On the side of each right hand page, there is an indication of the chords that are dealt with on the following page, the book deals with the complete range of chords as follows:- major, minor, augmented fifth, minor fifth, major sixth, minor sixth, dominant seventh, augmented ninth, minor seventh, thirteenth, with minor ninth, major seventh, diminished seventh, seventh and augmented fifth, seventh with minor fifth, ninth, minor ninth, ninth with augmented fifth, ninth with minor fifth, ninth with major seventh, eleventh with augmented eleventh, thirteenth.

Each graph consists of: a small staff with the notes of the chord and a section of the fingerboard in which are shown:-

With roman numerals - the first key of the position,
With arabic numerals - the fingering and under each fingerboard or fretboard the name of each note.

I take this opportunity to thank Mr. Adolfo de Carolis for his great help in achieving this book.

I also thank the Musical Publishing House of "Farfisa" for having undertaken its publication.

The Author

HOW TO READ CHORD DIAGRAMS IN THIS BOOK

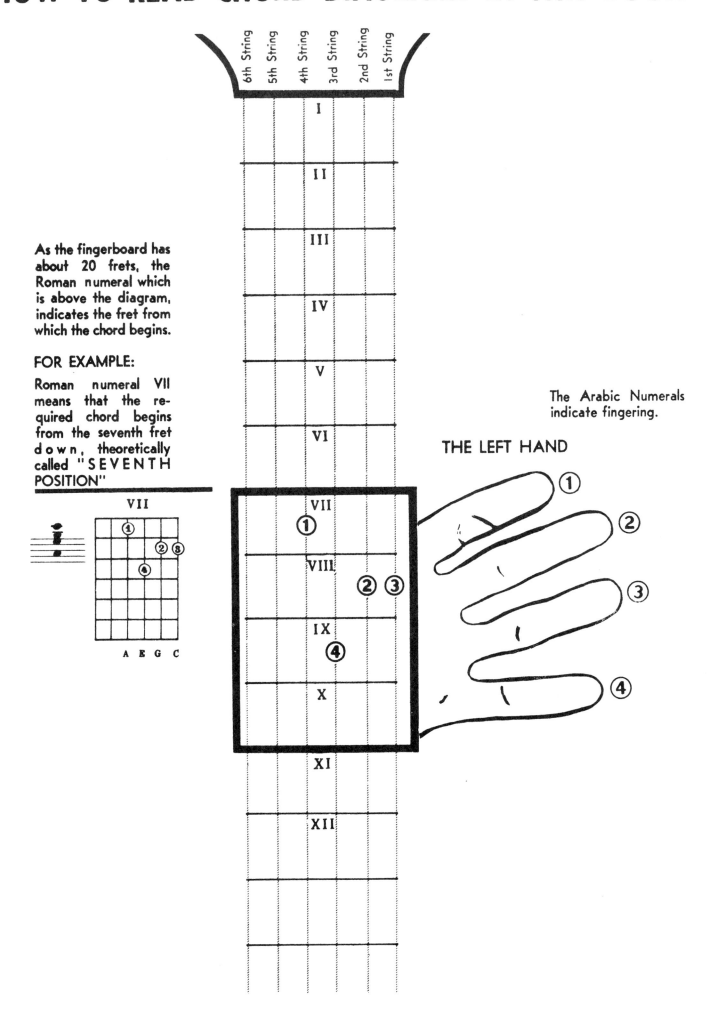

6th String · 5th String · 4th String · 3rd String · 2nd String · 1st String

I
II
III
IV
V
VI
VII
VIII
IX
X
XI
XII

As the fingerboard has about 20 frets, the Roman numeral which is above the diagram, indicates the fret from which the chord begins.

FOR EXAMPLE:

Roman numeral VII means that the required chord begins from the seventh fret down, theoretically called "SEVENTH POSITION"

VII

A E G C

The Arabic Numerals indicate fingering.

THE LEFT HAND

Index of Chords

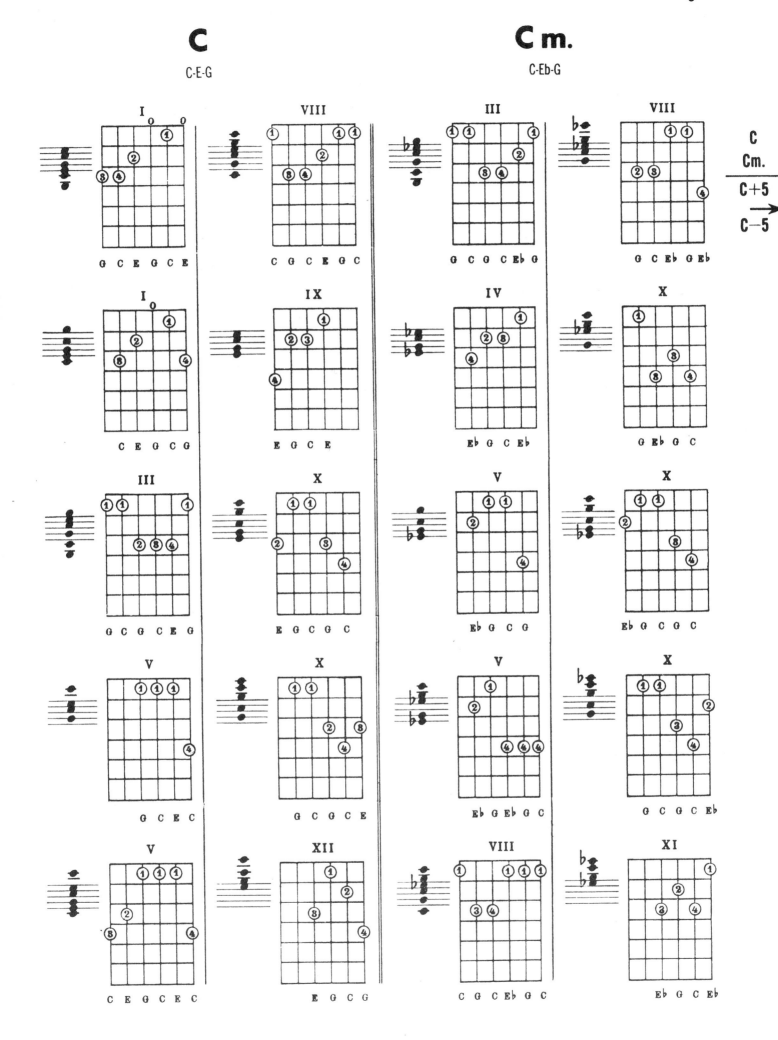

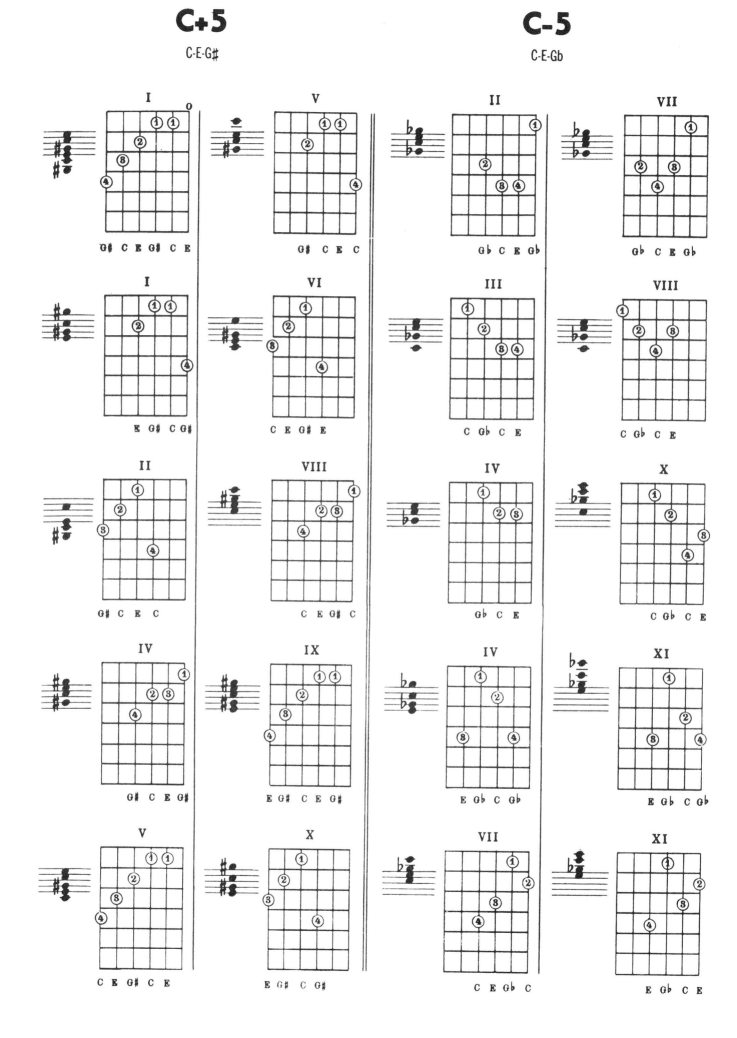

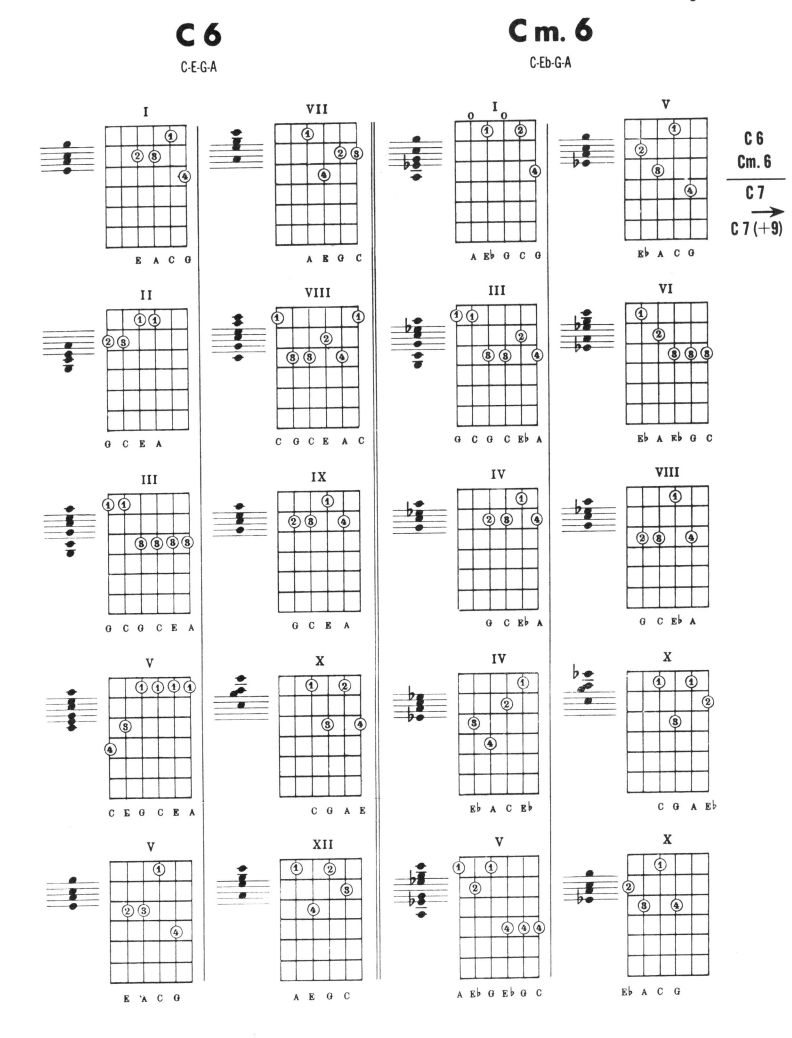

C7

C-E-G-Bb

C7 (+9)

C-E-G-Bb-D#

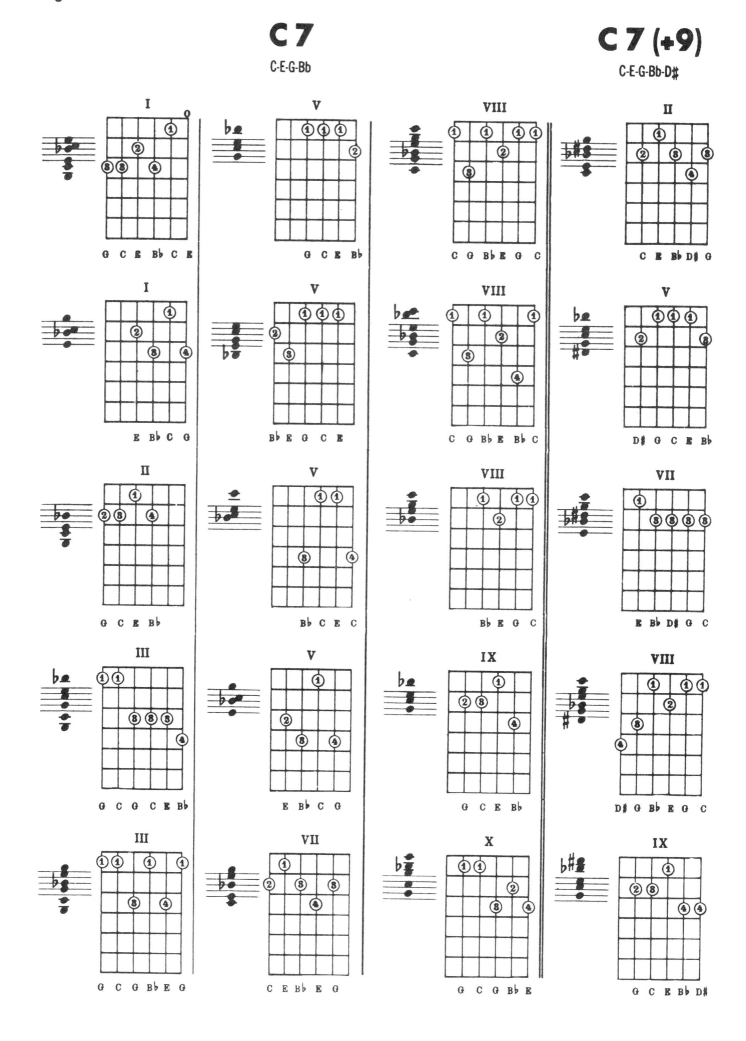

C m. 7

C-Eb-G-Bb

C 13 (-9)

C-G-Bb-Db-A

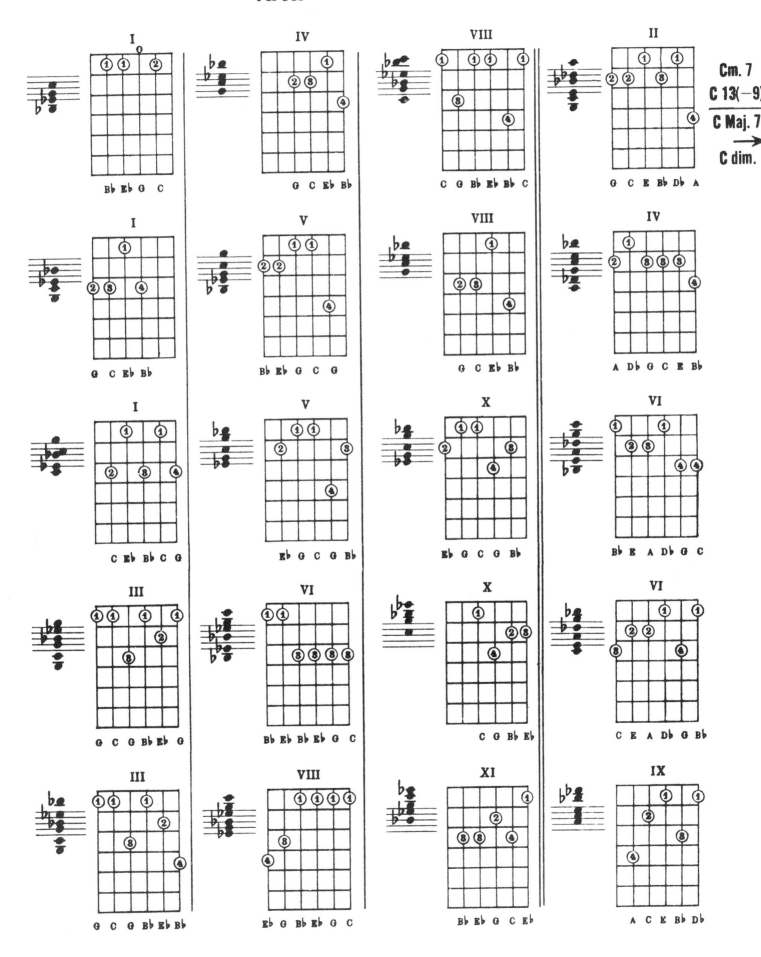

Cm. 7
C 13 (-9)
―――――
C Maj. 7
→
C dim.

C maj. 7
C-E-G-B

C dim.
C-Eb-Gb-Bbb

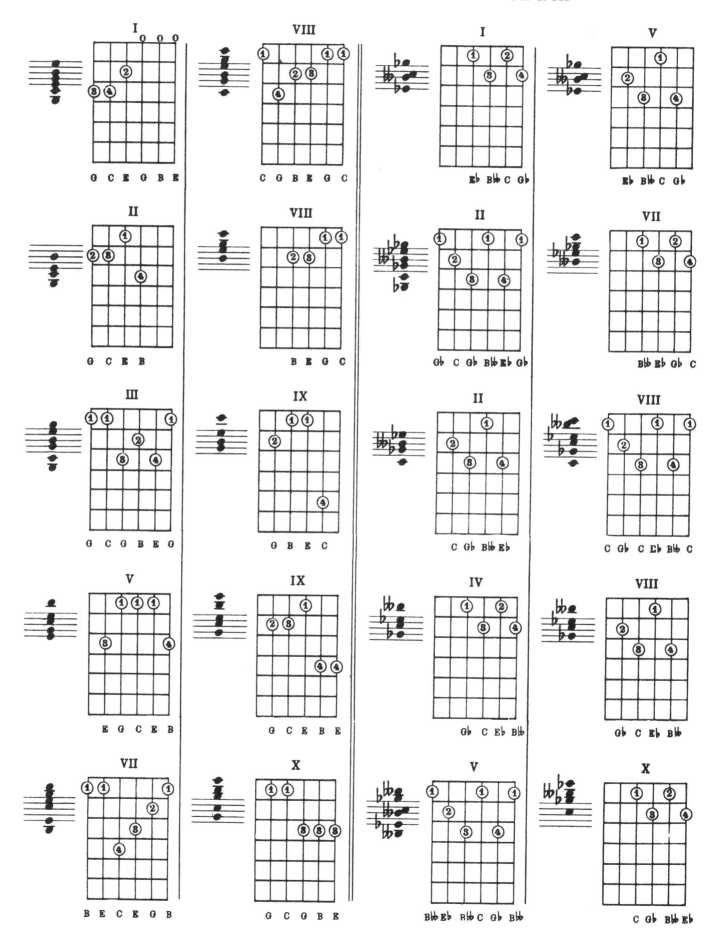

C 7 (+5)
C-E-G#-Bb

C 7 (-5)
C-E-Gb-Bb

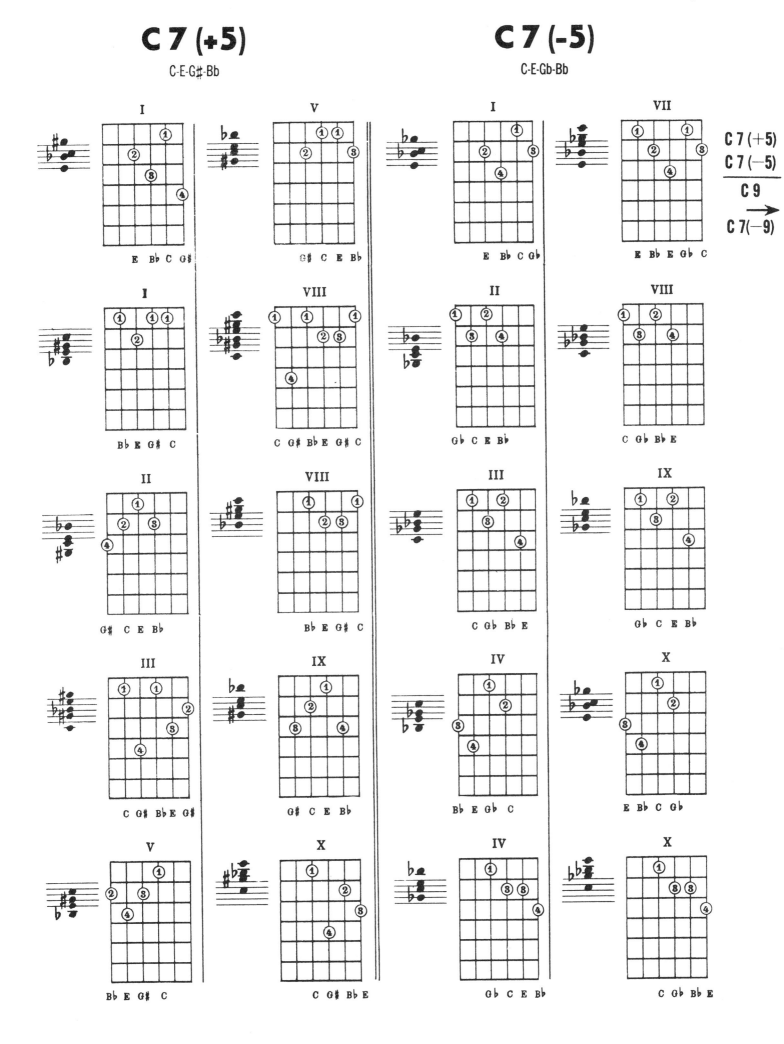

C 7 (+5)
C 7 (−5)
C 9
C 7 (−9)

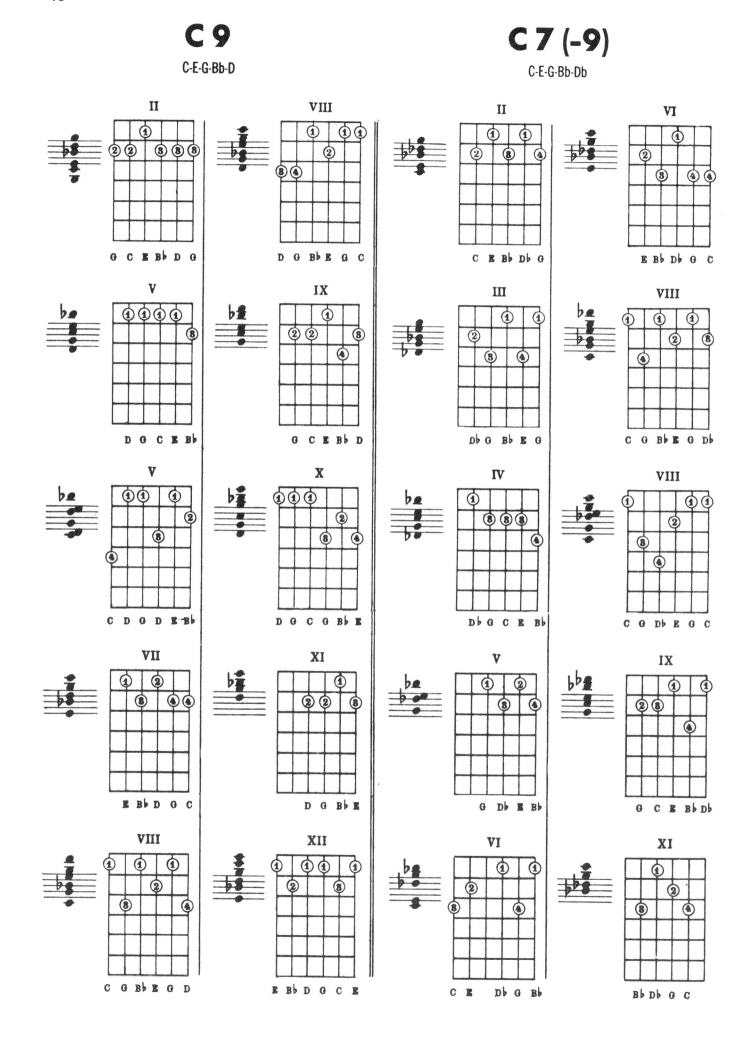

C 9 (+5)
C·E·G#·Bb·D

C 9 (-5)
C·E·Gb·Bb·D

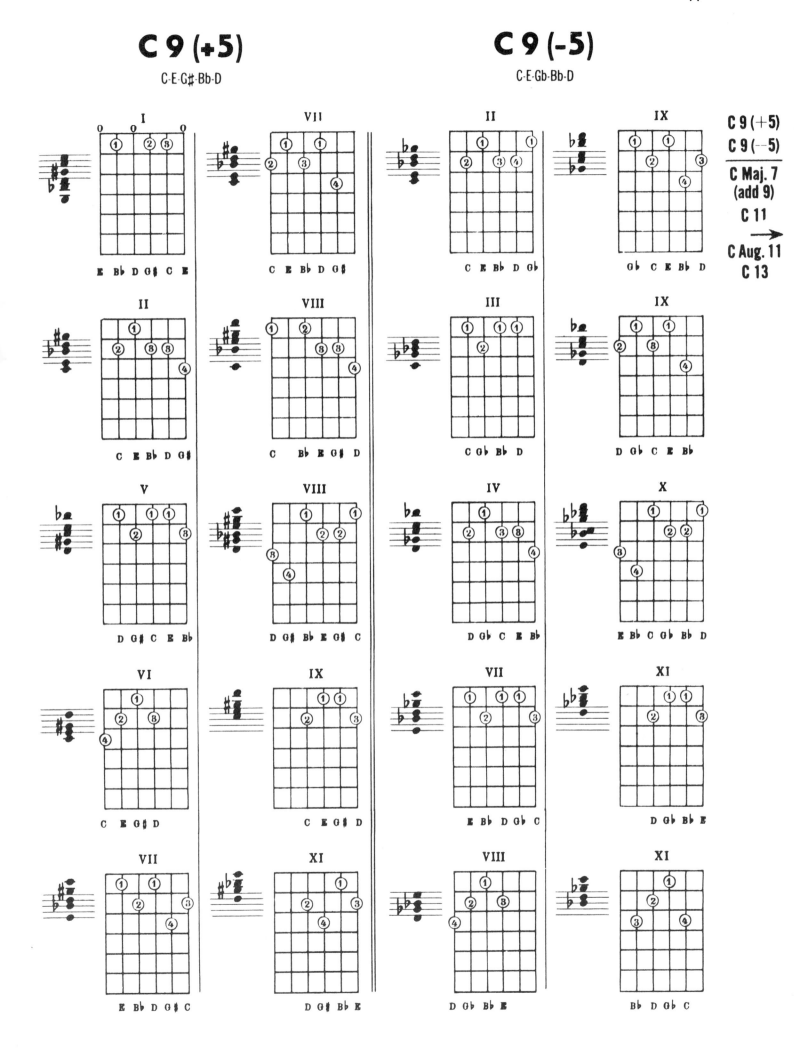

C 9 (+5)
C 9 (—5)
C Maj. 7 (add 9)
C 11
→
C Aug. 11
C 13

C maj. 7 (add 9)
C-E-G-B-D

C 11
C-E-G-Bb-D-F

C aug. 11
C-E-G-Bb-D-F♯

C 13
C-E-G-Bb-D-A

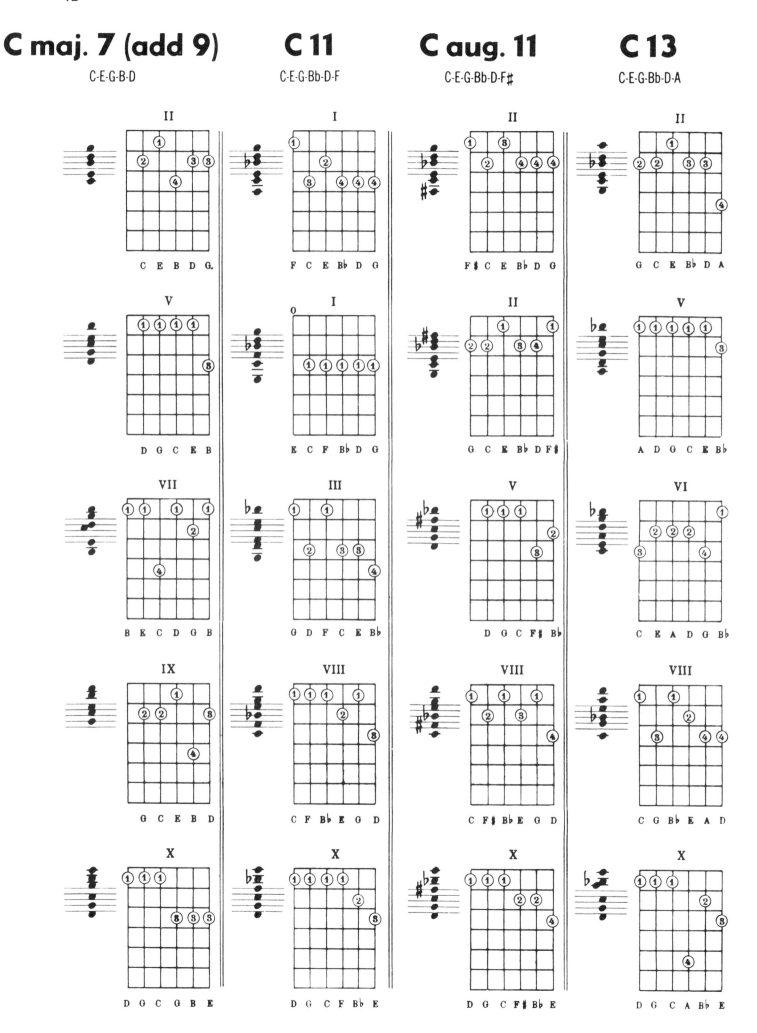

Db or C#

Db-F-Ab   C#-E#-G#

Db m. or C# m.

Db-Fb-Ab   C#-E-G#

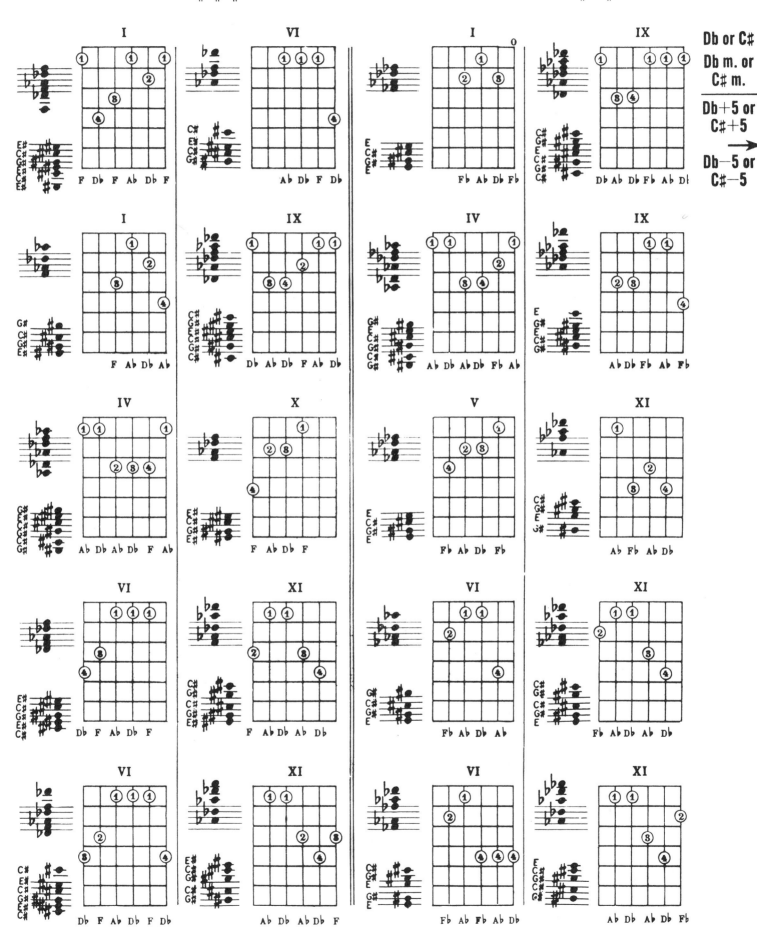

Db or C#
Db m. or
C# m.
_____
Db+5 or
C#+5
→
Db−5 or
C#−5

Db+5 or C#+5

Db-F-A   C#-E#-A

Db-5 or C#-5

Db-F-Abb   C#-E#-G

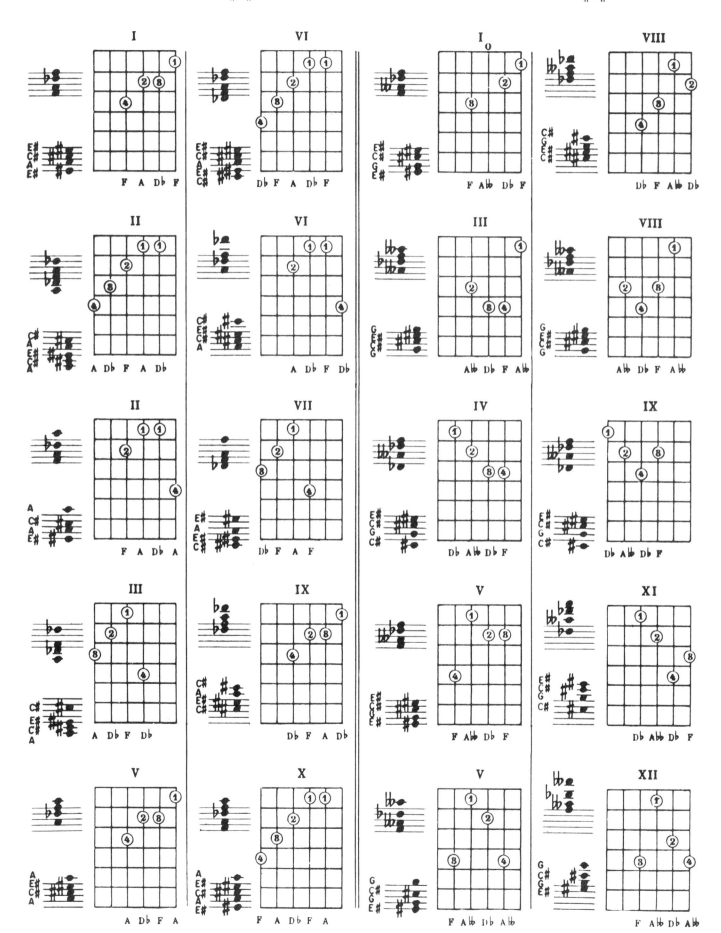

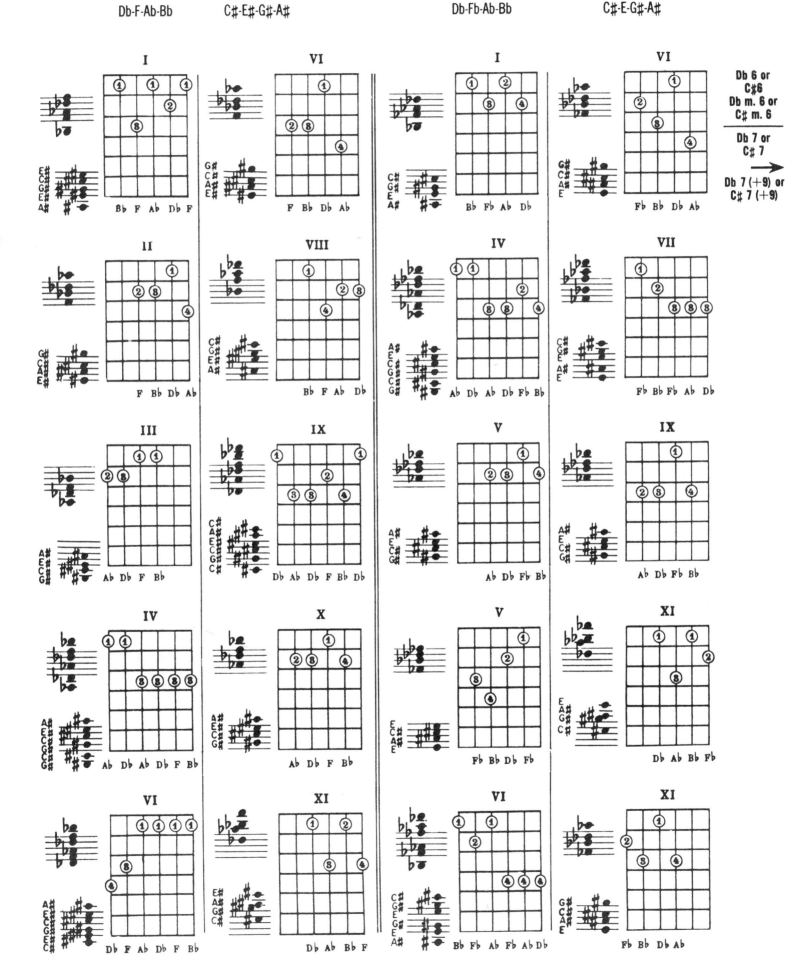

16

Db 7 or C# 7

Db-F-Ab-Cb   C#-E#-G#-B

Db 7 (+9)

Db-F-Ab-Cb-E

or

C# 7 (+9)

C#-E#-G#-B-Dx

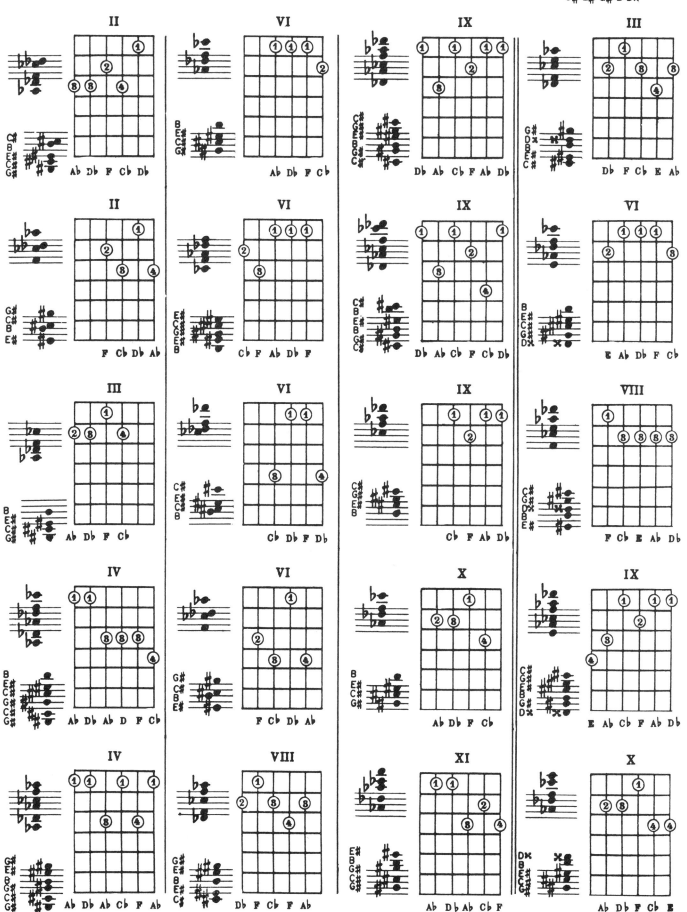

Db m. 7 or C# m. 7

Db-Fb-Ab-Cb   C#-E-G#-B

Db 13 (-9) or C# 13 (-9)

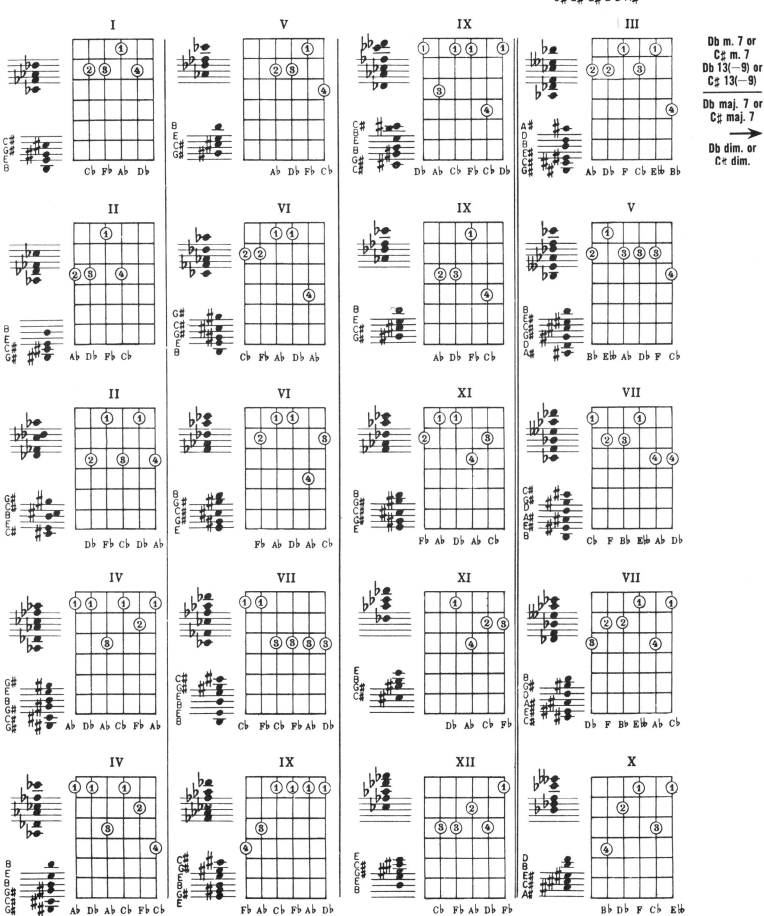

Db-F-Ab-Cb-Ebb-Bb

C#-E#-G#-B-D-A#

Db m. 7 or
C# m. 7
Db 13(—9) or
C# 13(—9)

Db maj. 7 or
C# maj. 7
→

Db dim. or
C# dim.

Db maj. 7 or C# maj. 7

Db-F-A-Ab-C   C#-E#-G#-B#

Db dim. or C# dim.

Db-Fb-Abb-Cbb   C#-E-G-Bb

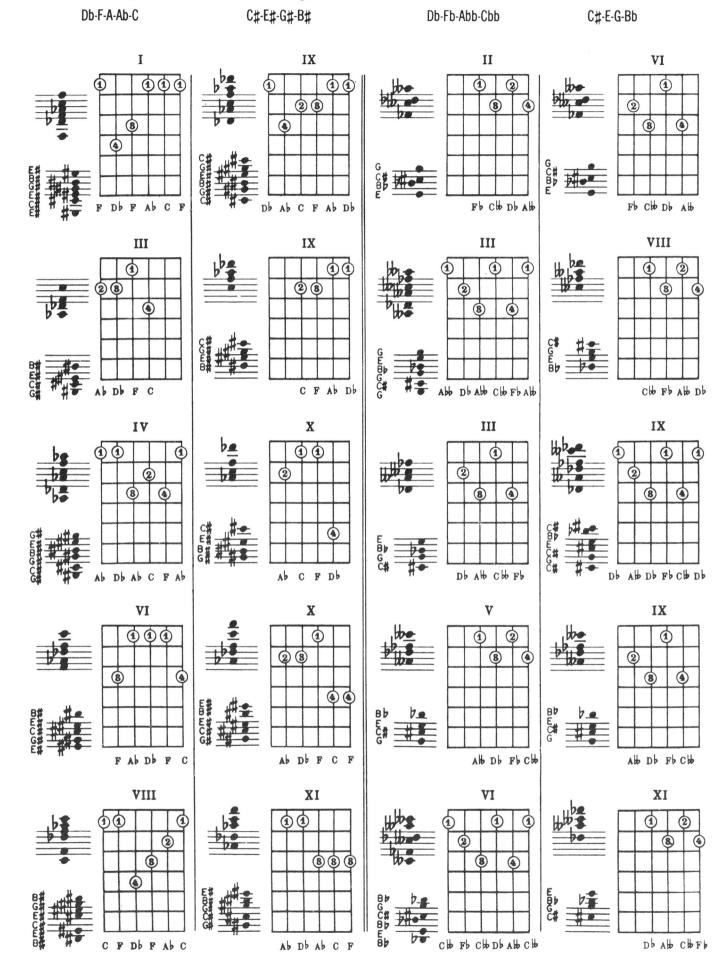

Db 7 (+5) or C# 7 (+5)

Db-F-A-Cb   C#-E#-Gx-B

Db 7 (-5) or C# 7 (-5)

Db-F-Abb-Cb   C#-E#-G-B

20

Db 9   or   C# 9

Db-F-Ab-Cb-Eb   C#-E#-G#-B-D#

Db 7 (-9) or C# 7 (-9)

Db-F-Ab-Cb-Ebb   C#-E#-G#-B-D

Db 9 (+5) or C# 9 (+5)

Db-F-A-Cb-Eb   C#-E#-Gx-B-D#

Db 9 (-5) or C# 9 (-5)

Db-F-Abb-Cb-Eb   C#-E#-G-B-D#

Db 9 (+5) or
C# 9 (+5)
Db 9 (−5) or
C# 9 (−5)
Db maj. 7
(add 9) or
C# maj. 7
(add 9)
Db 11 or
C# 11

Db aug.11 or
C# aug. 11
Db 13 or
C# 13

Db maj. 7 (add 9)

Db-F-Ab-C-Eb

or

C# maj. 7 (add 9)

C#-E#-G#-B#-D#

Db 11

Db-F-Ab-Cb-Eb-Gb

or

C# 11

C#-E#-G#-B-D#-F#

Db aug. 11

Db-F-Ab-Cb-Eb-G

or

C# aug. 11

C#-E#-G#-B-D#-Fx

Db 13

Db-F-Ab-Cb-Eb-Bb

or

C# 13

C#-E#-G#-B-D#-A#

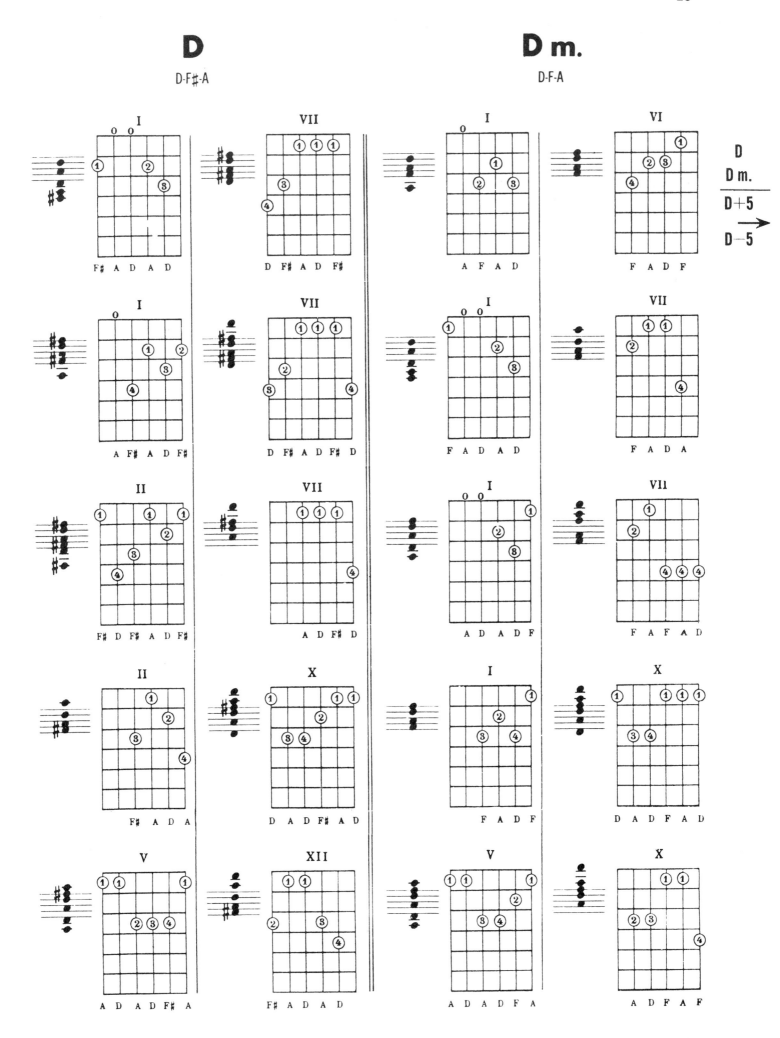

D+5
D-F#-A#

D-5
D-F#-Ab

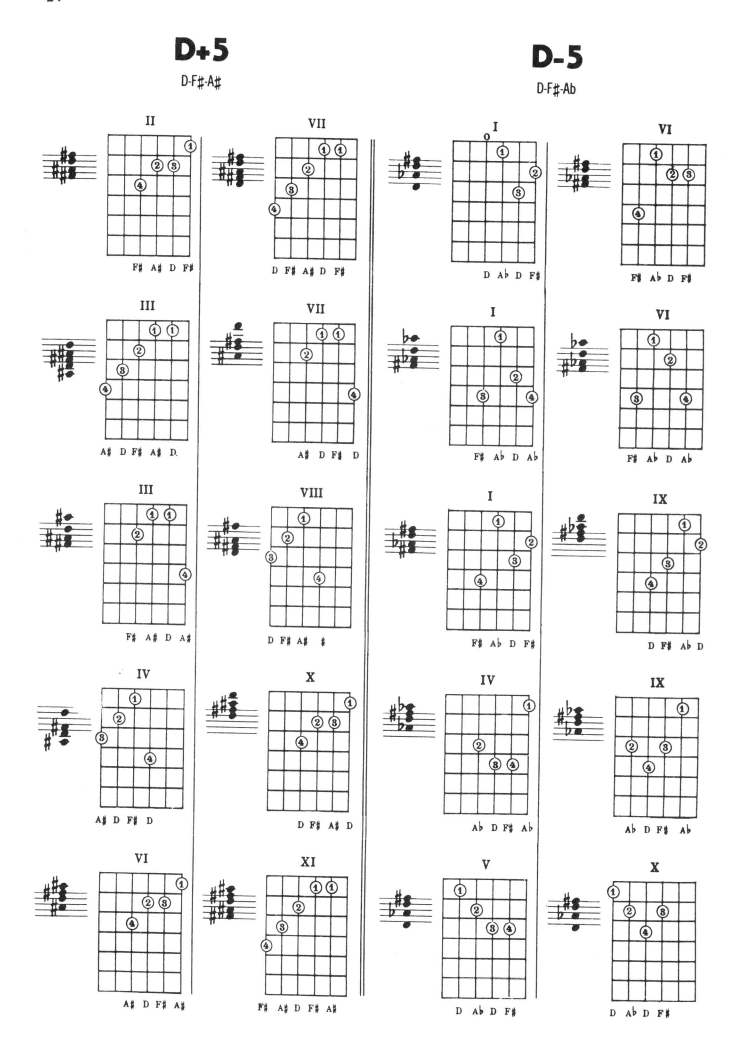

D 6

D-F#-A-B

Dm. 6

D-F-A-B

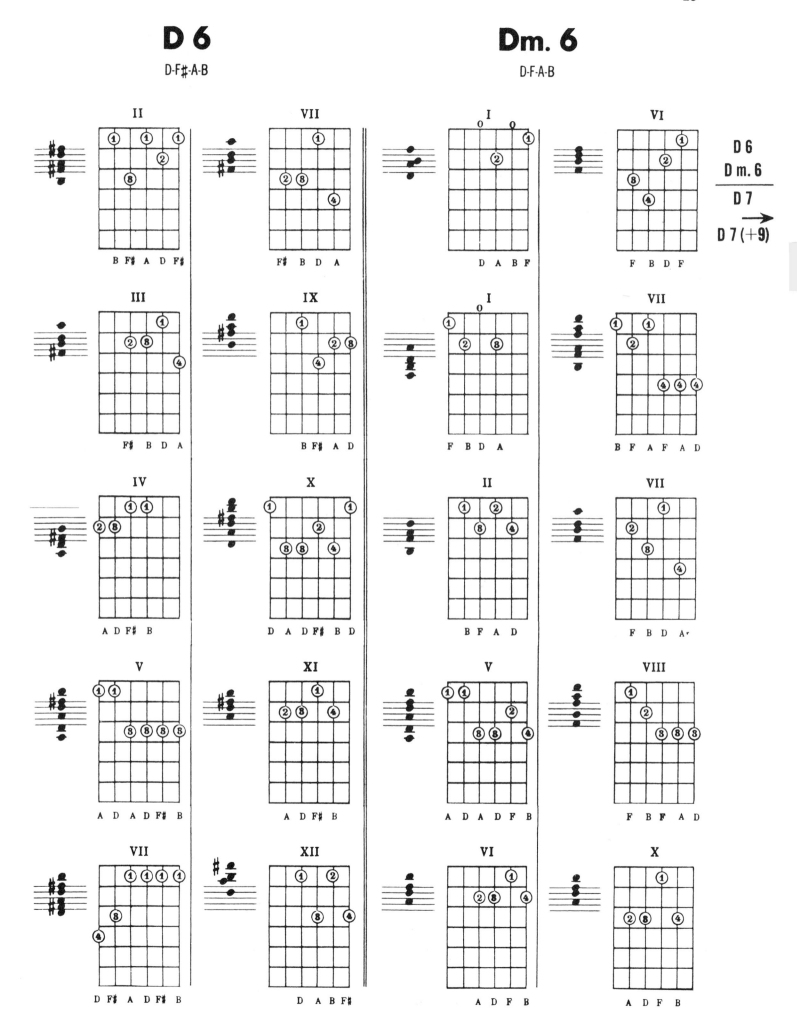

D 6
Dm. 6

D 7

D 7 (+9)

D 7
D-F#-A-C

D 7 (+9)
D-F#-A-C-E#

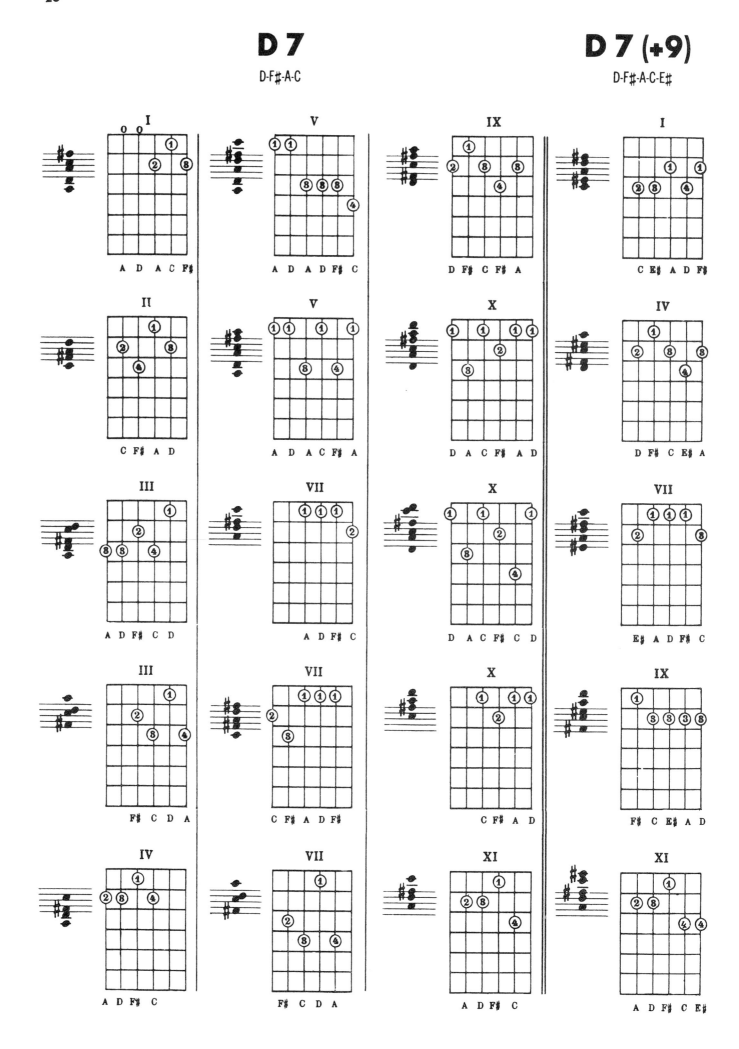

27

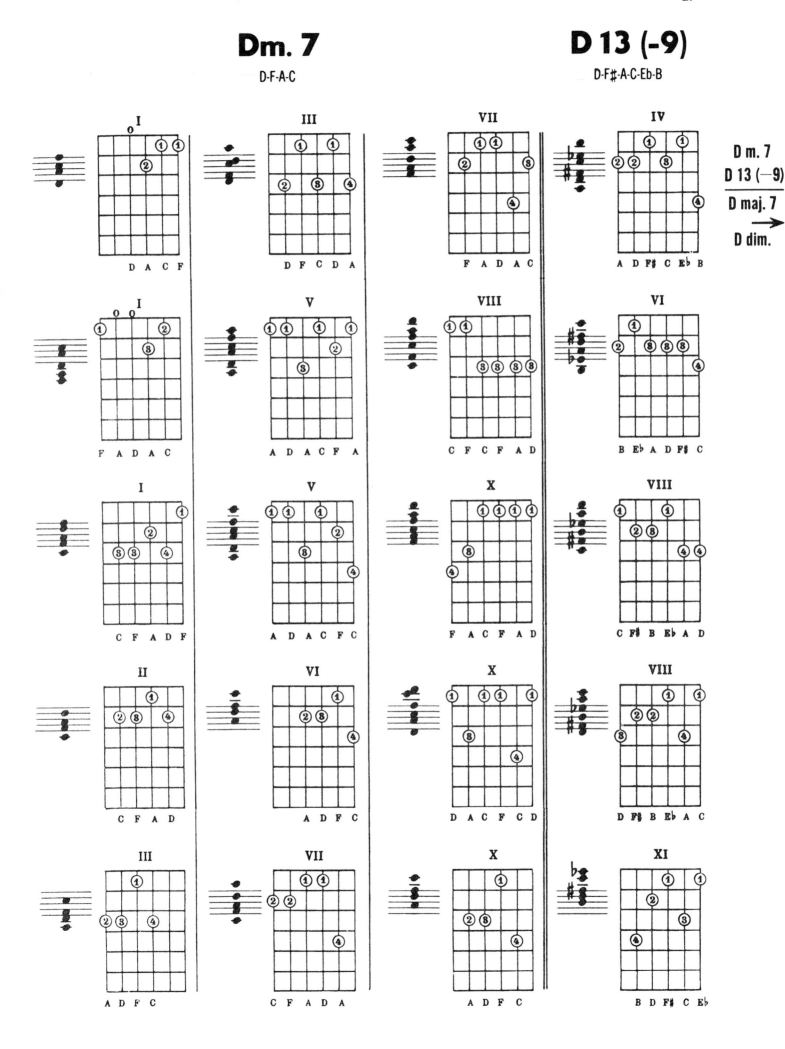

D maj. 7

D-F#-A-C#

D dim.

D-F-Ab-Cb

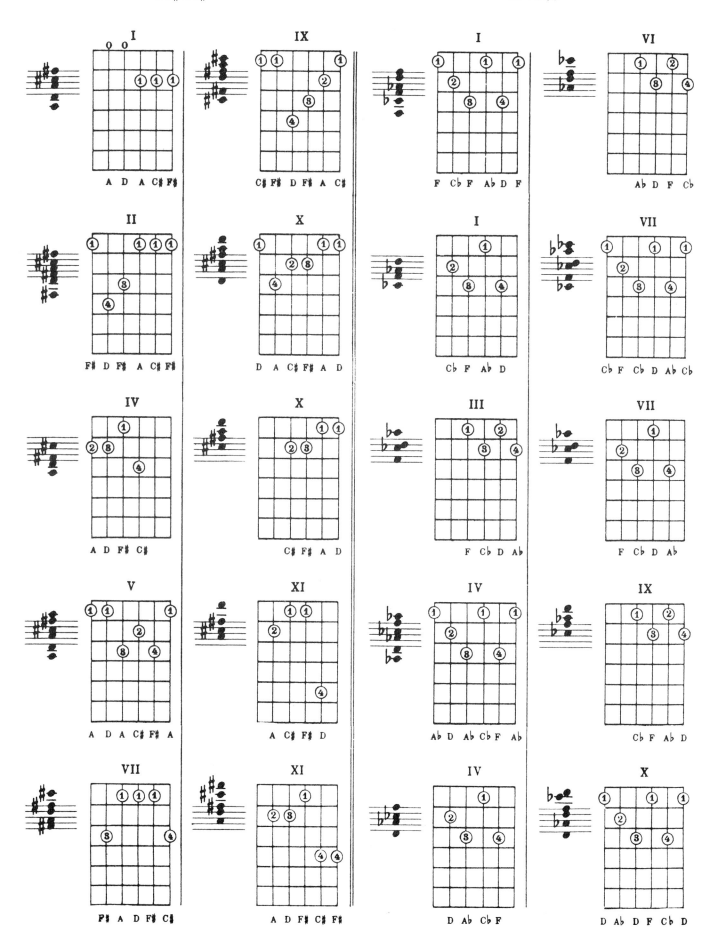

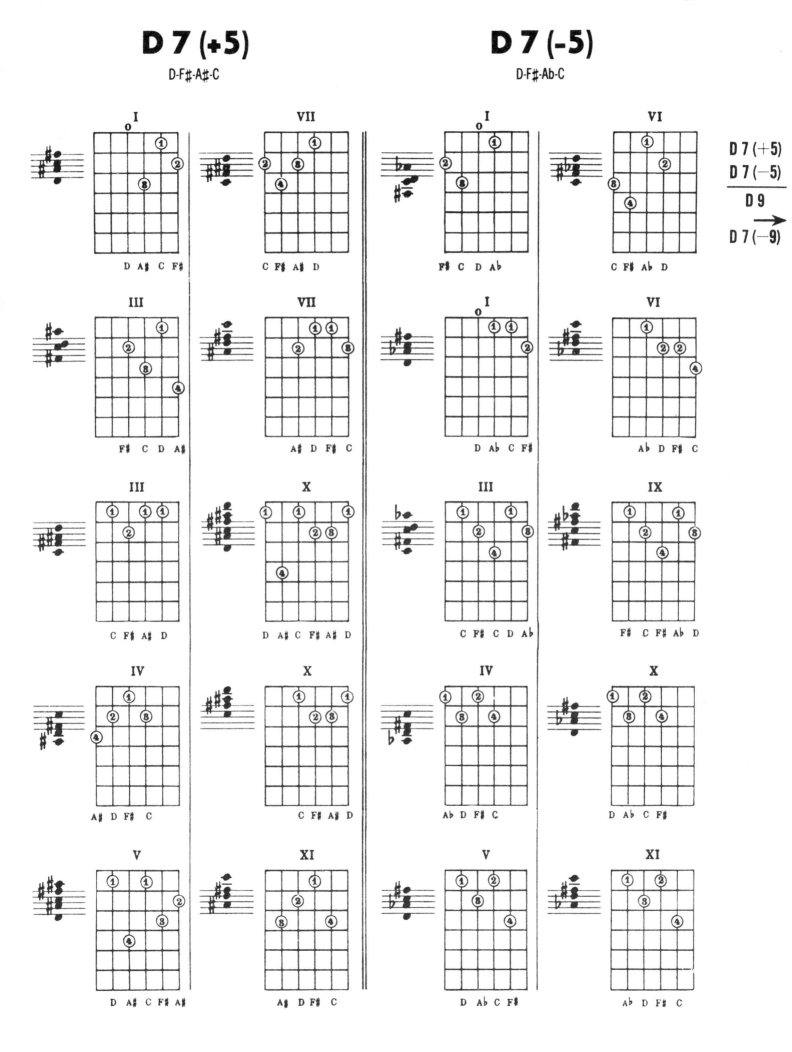

D 9

D-F♯-A-C-E

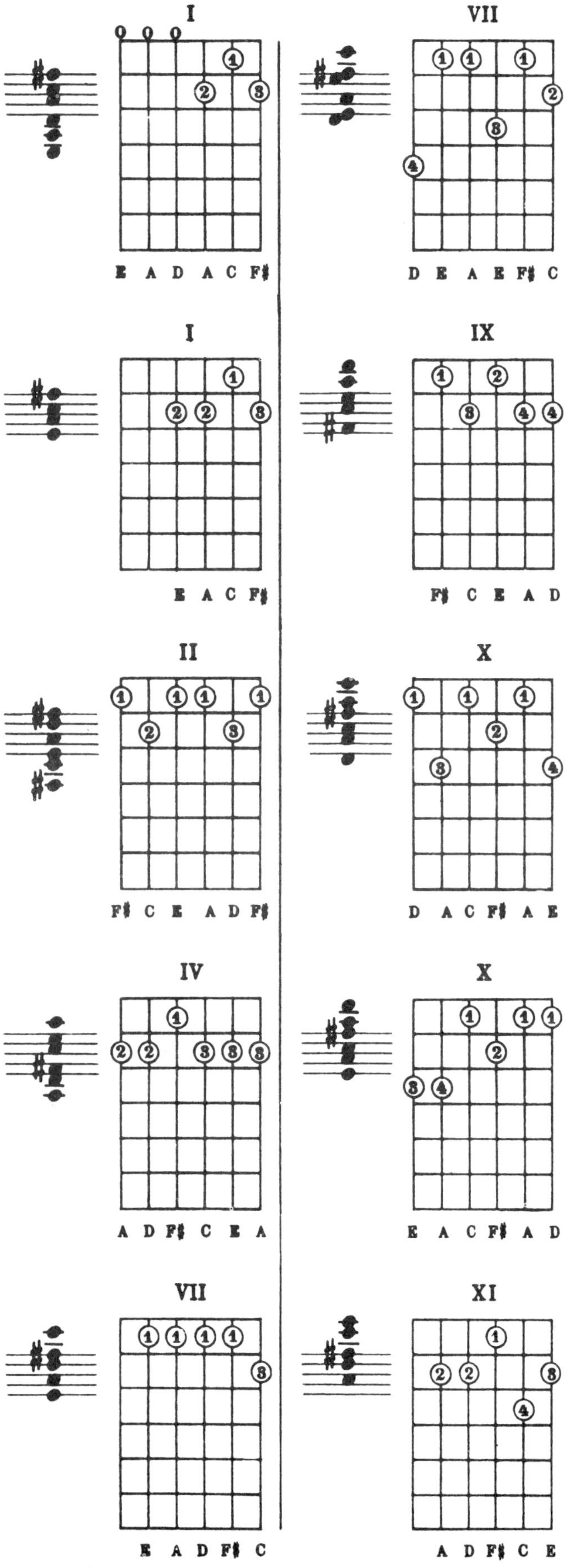

D 7 (-9)

D-F♯-A-C-Eb

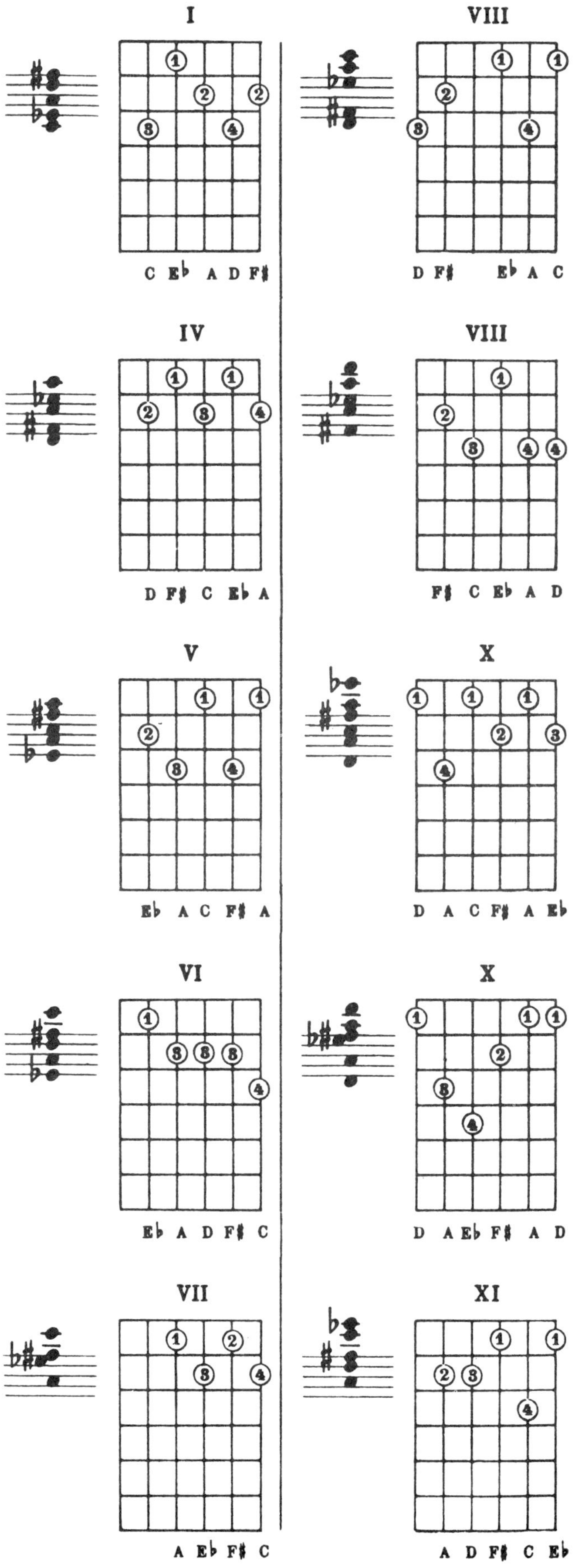

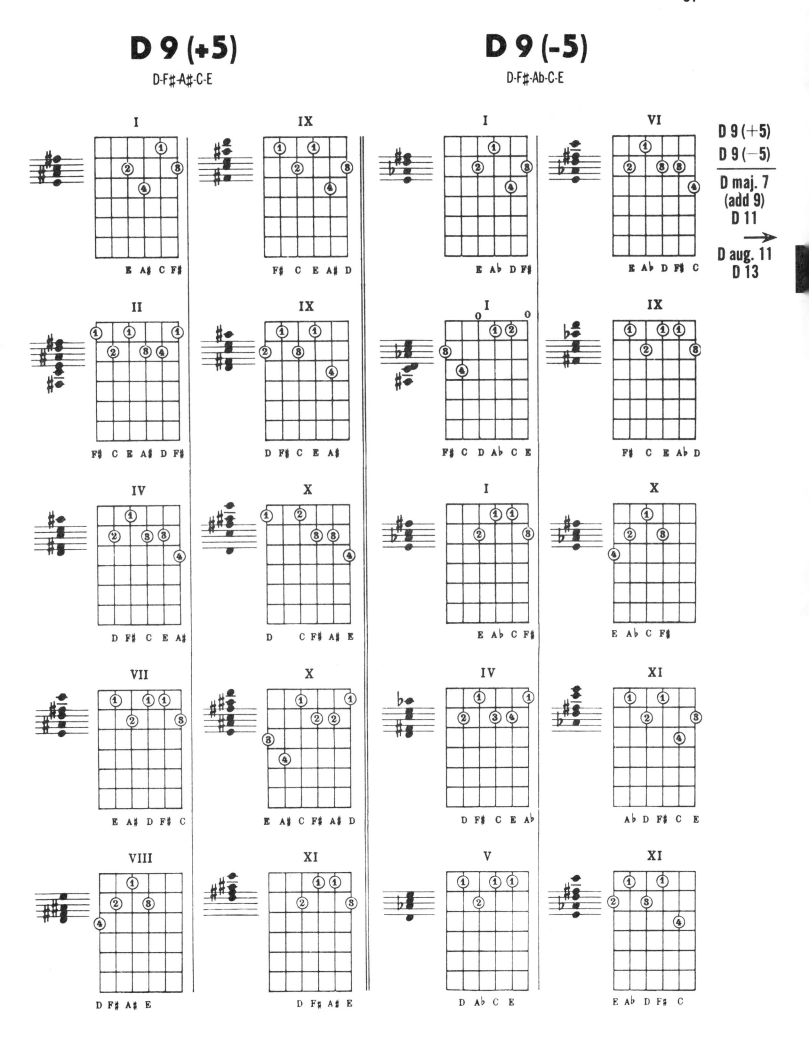

32

D maj. 7 (add 9)
D-F#-A-C#-E

D 11
D-F#-A-C-E-G

D aug. 11
D-F#-A-C-E-G#

D 13
D-F#-A-C-E-B

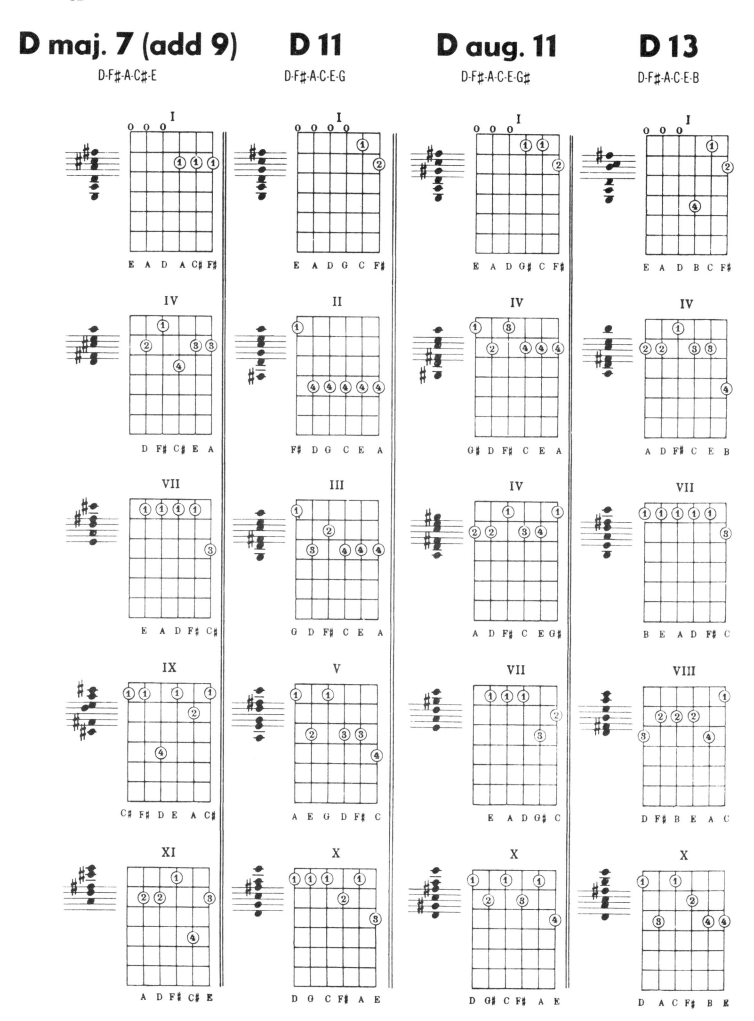

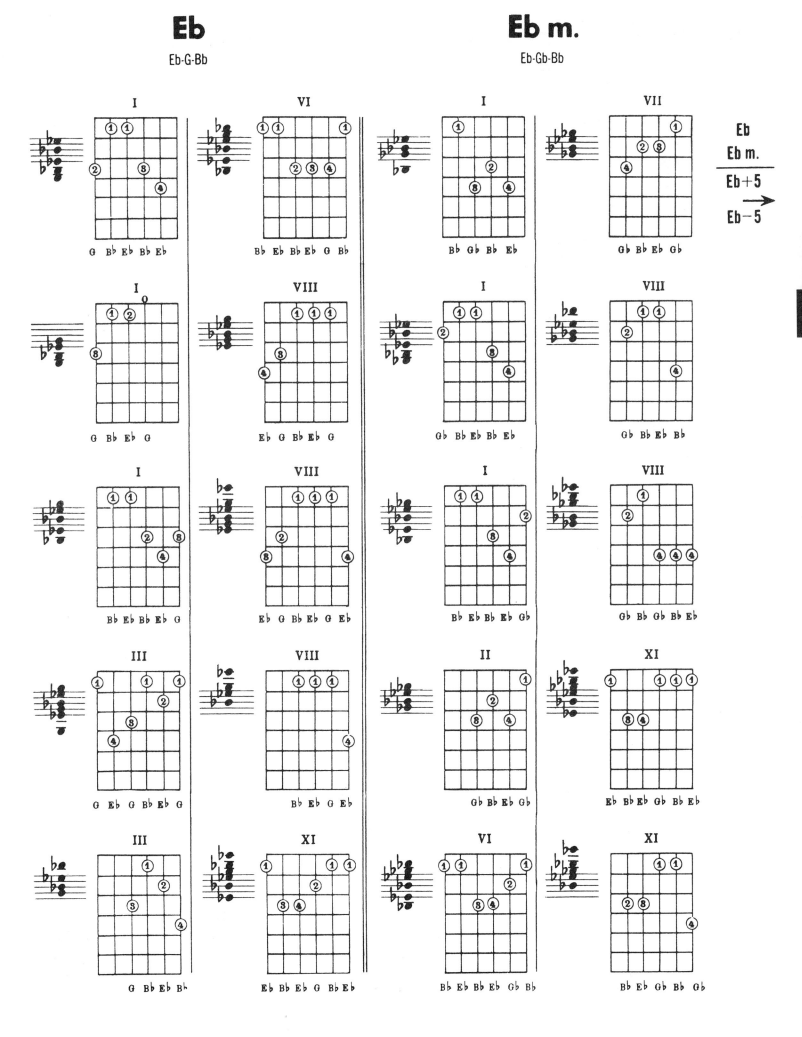

Eb+5
Eb-G-B

Eb-5
Eb-G-Bbb

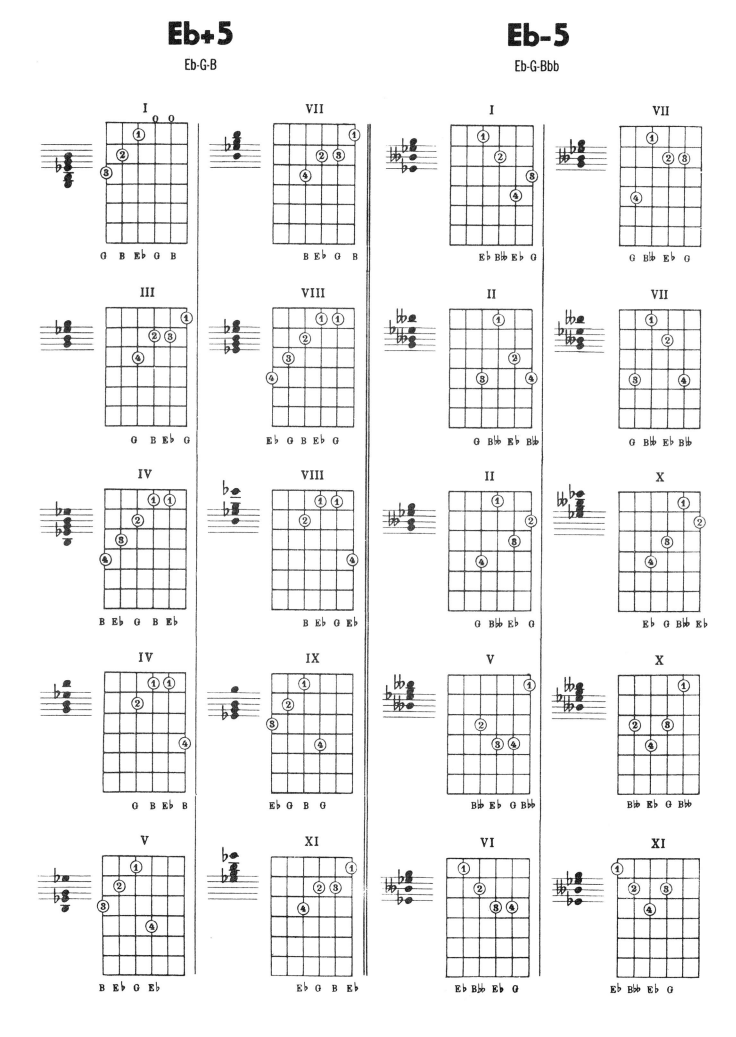

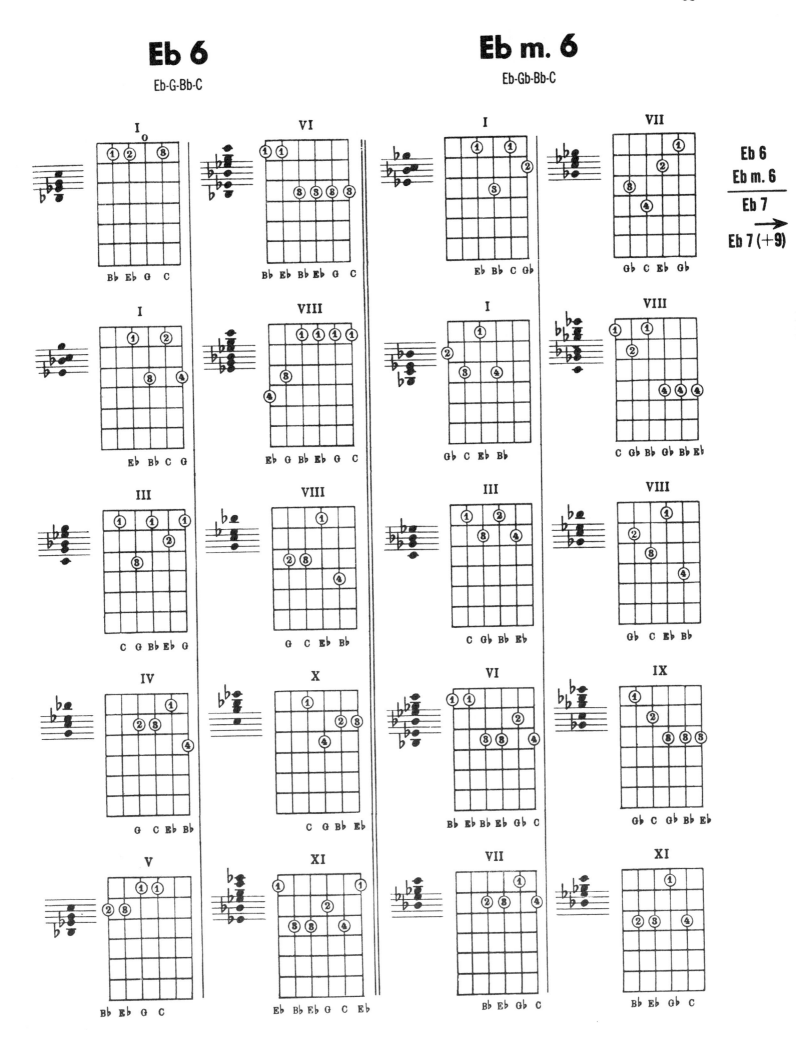

Eb 7

Eb-G-Bb-Db

Eb 7 (+9)

Eb-G-Bb-Db-F#

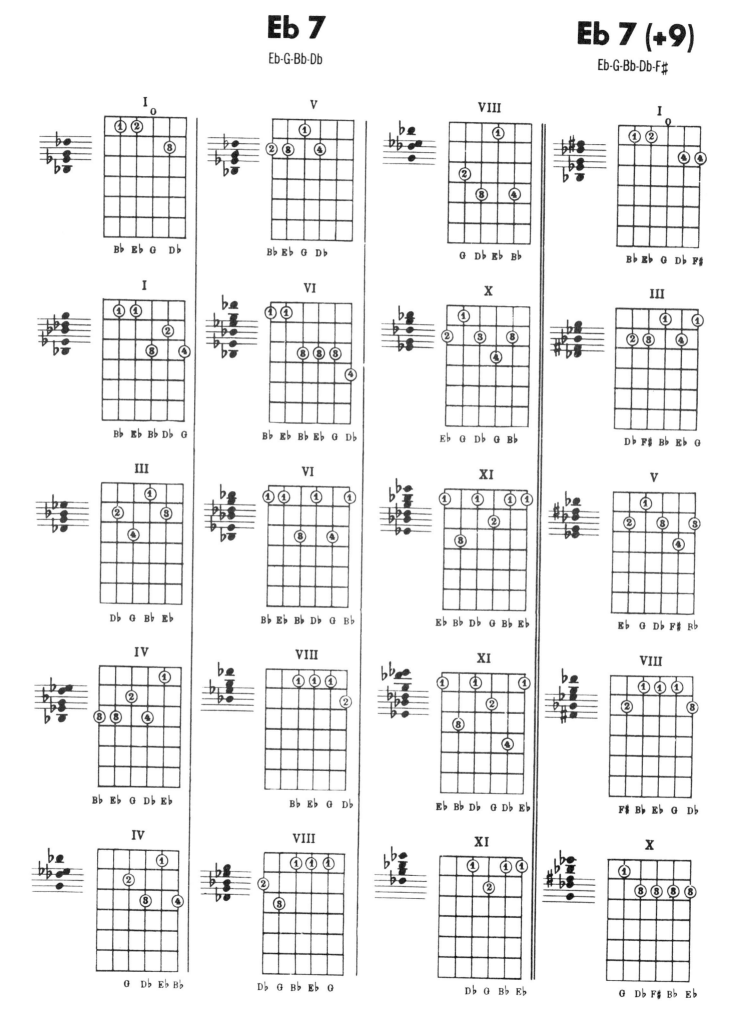

Eb m. 7

Eb-Gb-Bb-Db

Eb 13 (-9)

Eb-G-Bb-Db-Fb-C

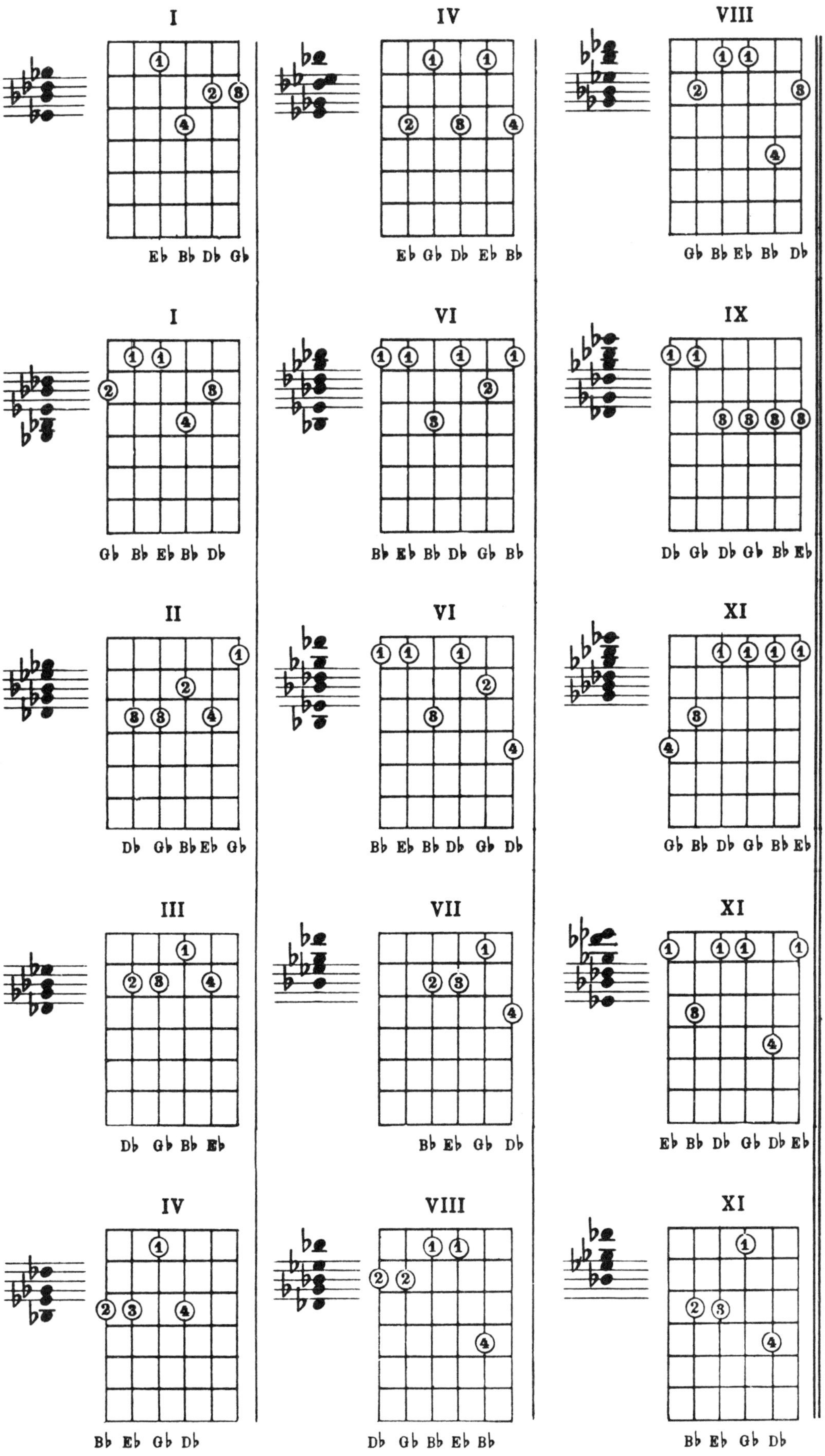

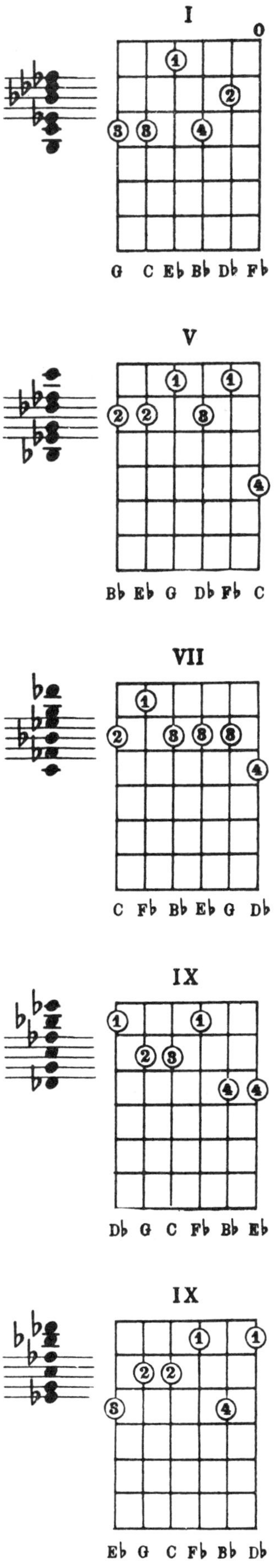

Eb m. 7
Eb 13(—9)
Eb maj. 7
→
Eb dim.

Eb maj. 7

Eb-G-Bb-D

Eb dim.

Eb-Gb-Bbb-Dbb

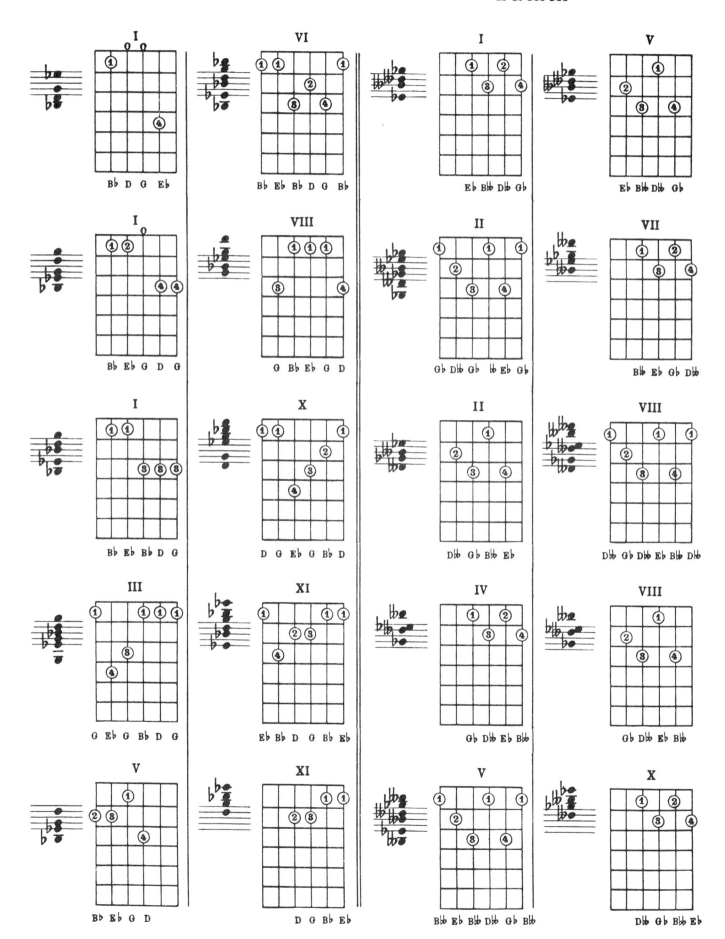

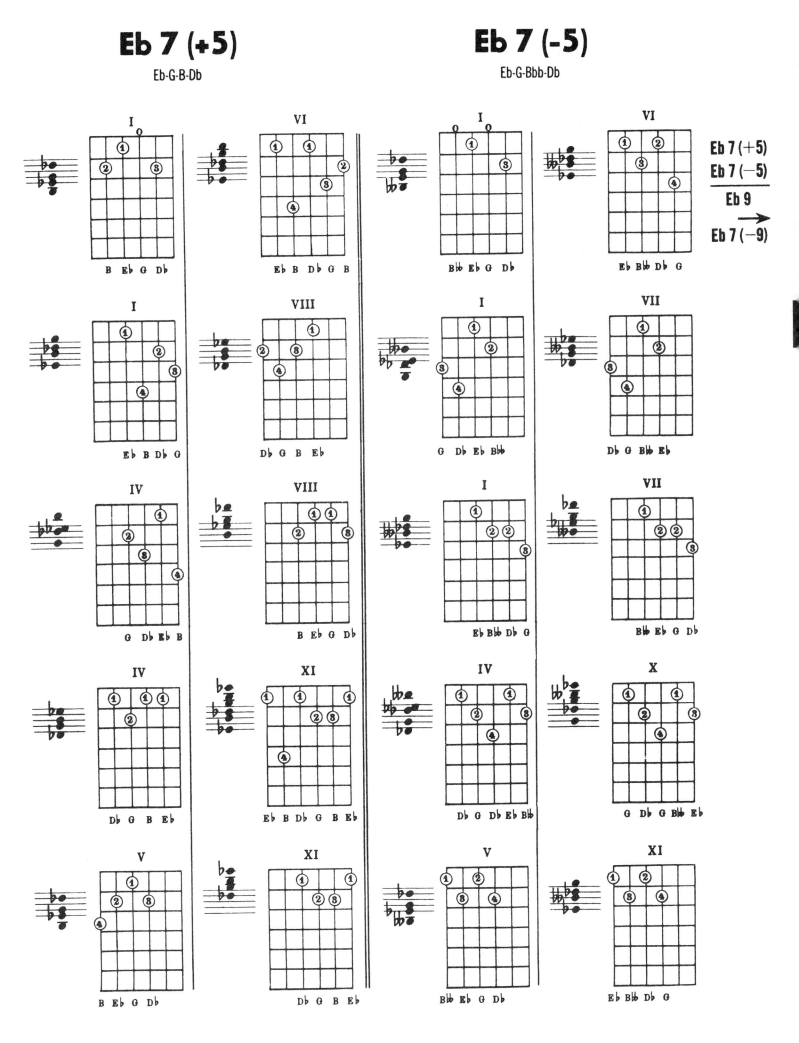

Eb 9

Eb-G-Bb-Db-F

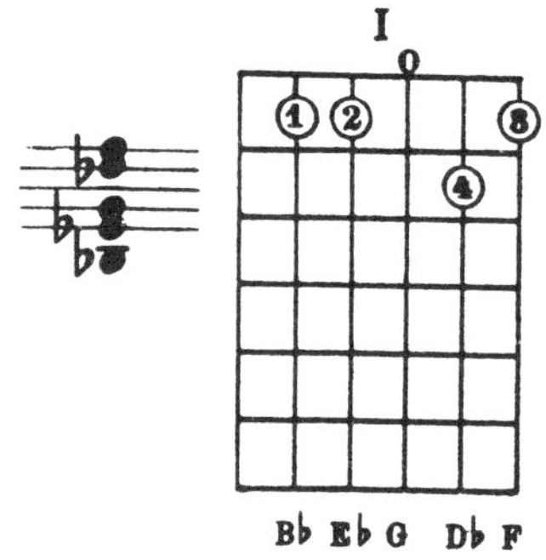

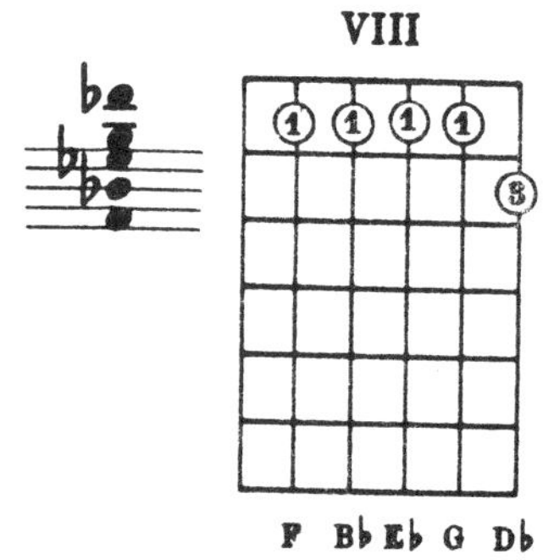

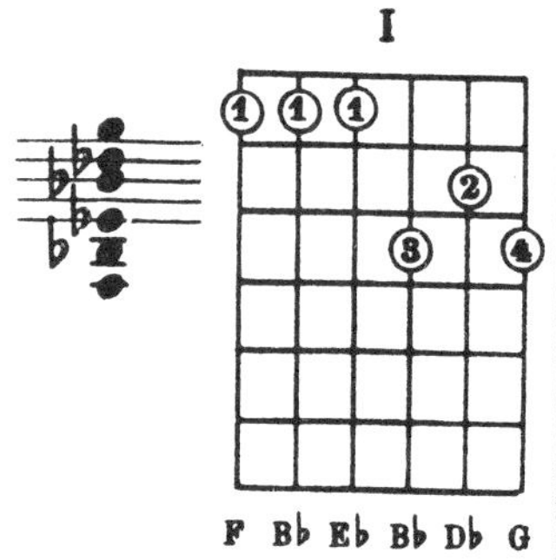

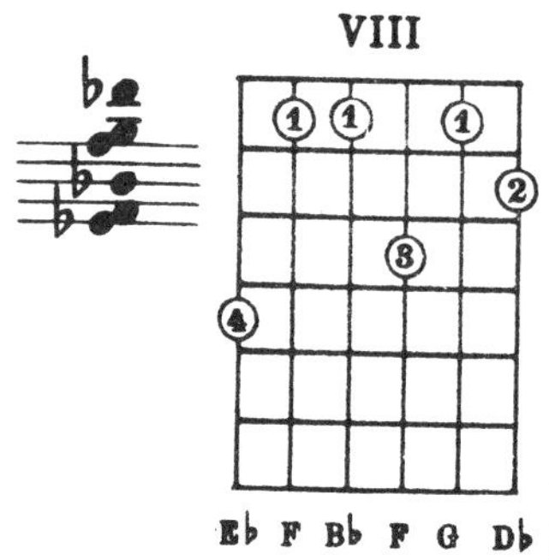

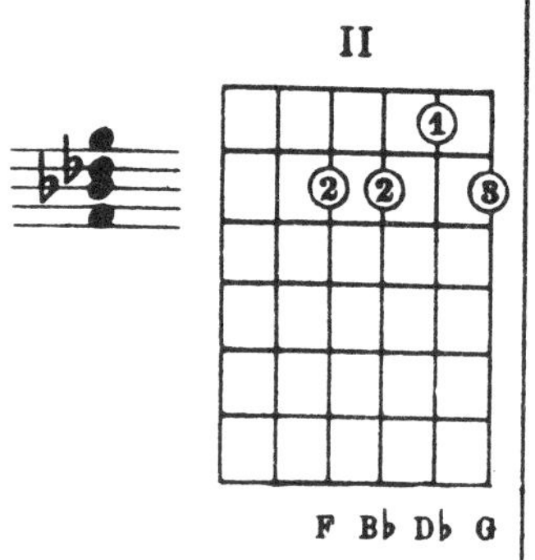

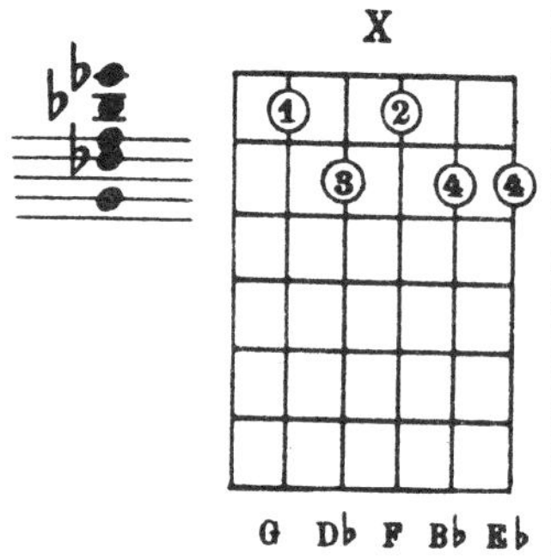

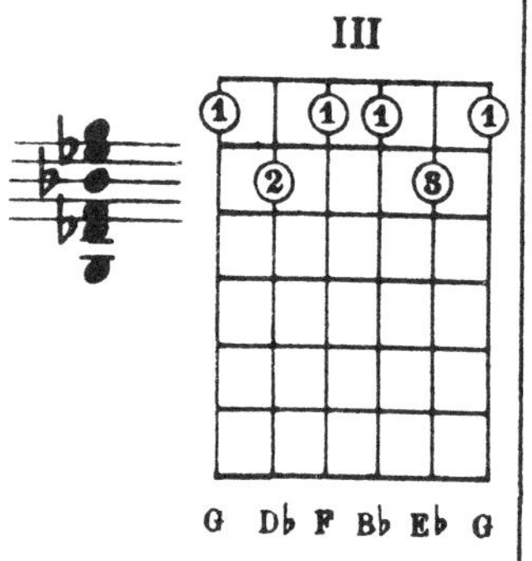

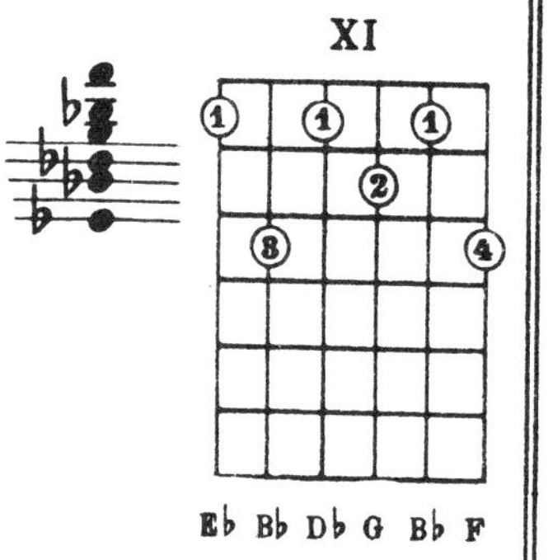

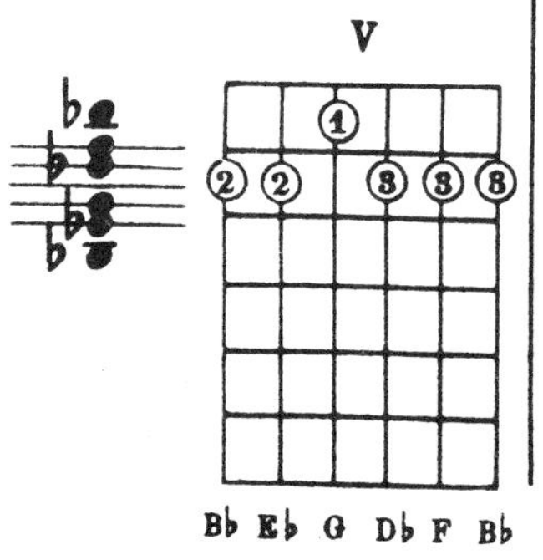

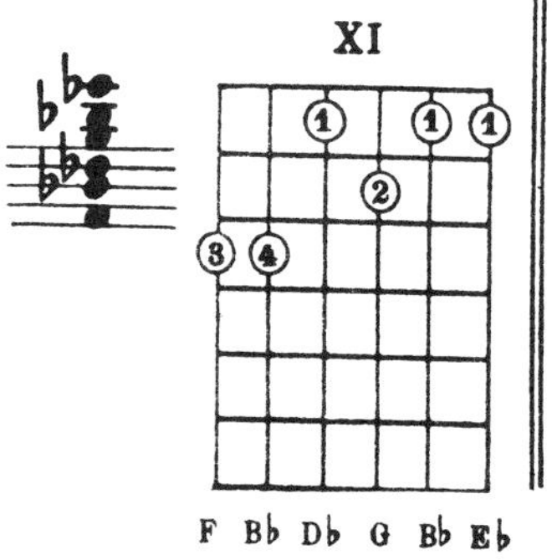

Eb 7 (-9)

Eb-G-Bb-Db-Fb

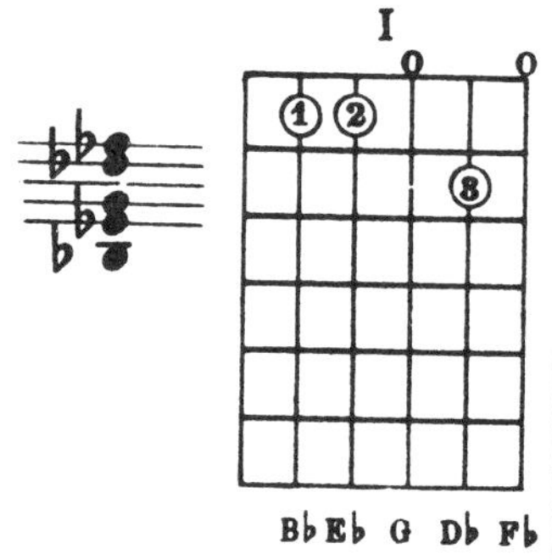

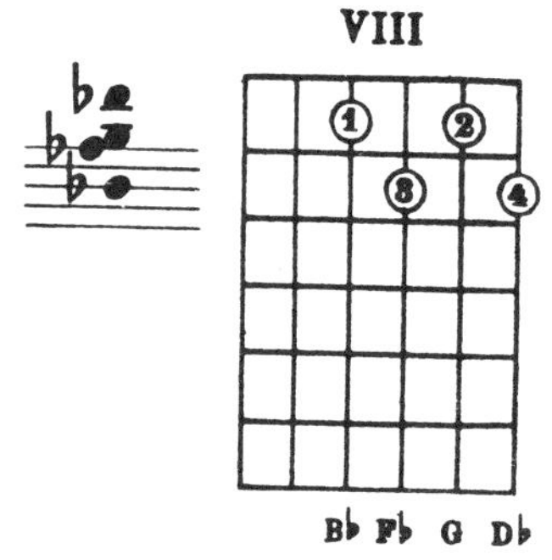

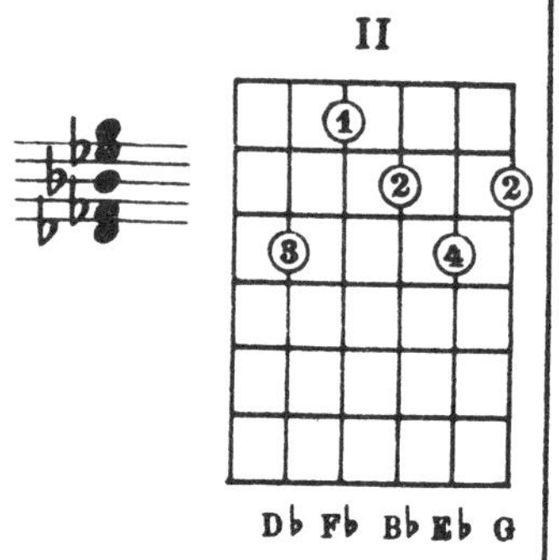

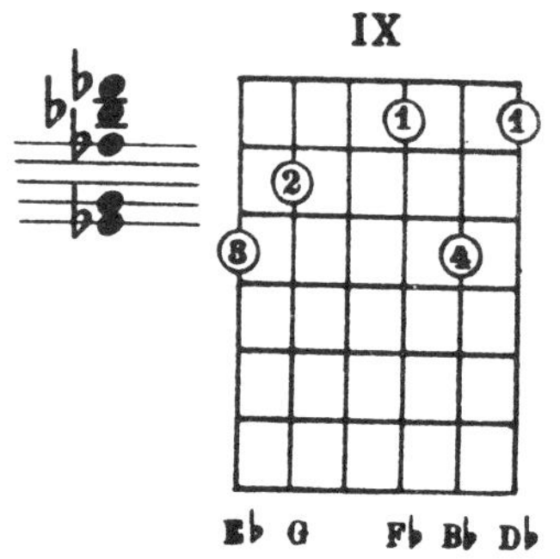

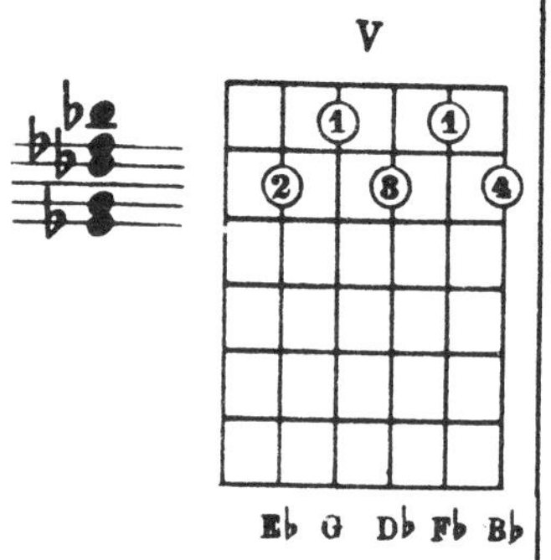

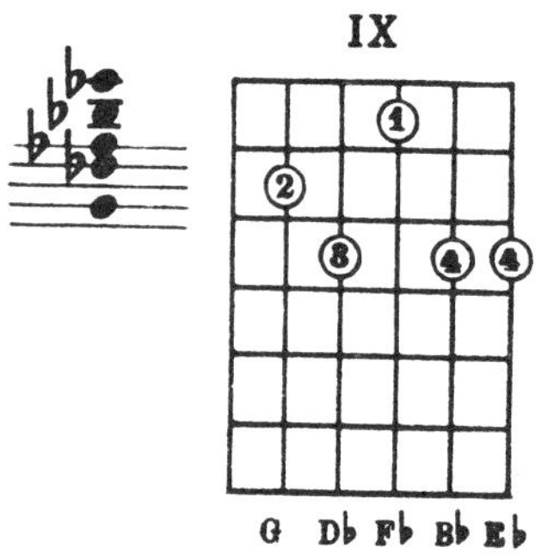

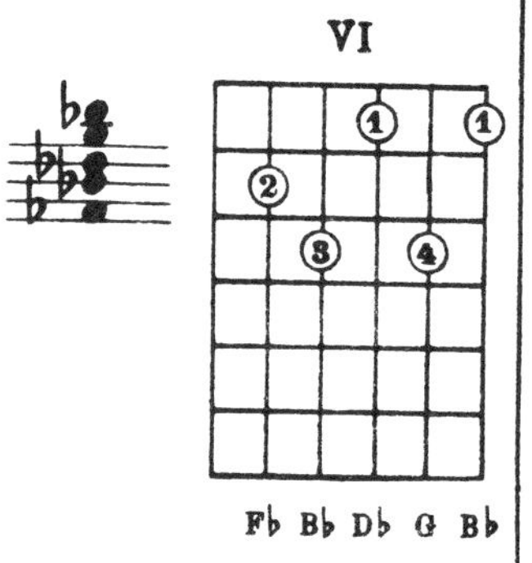

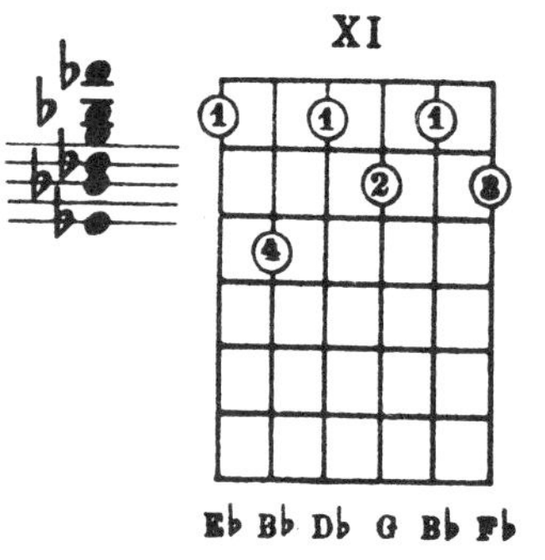

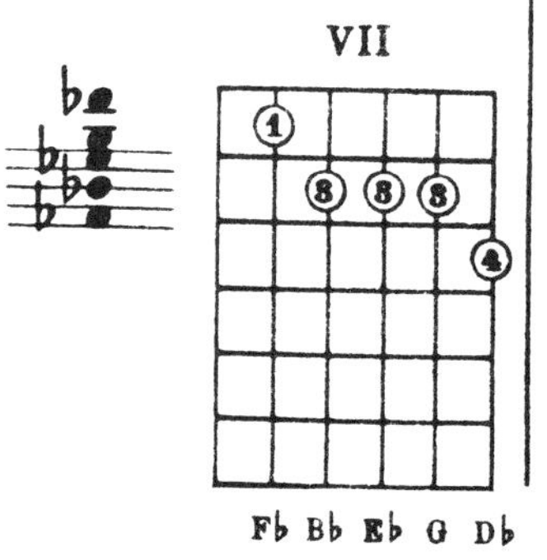

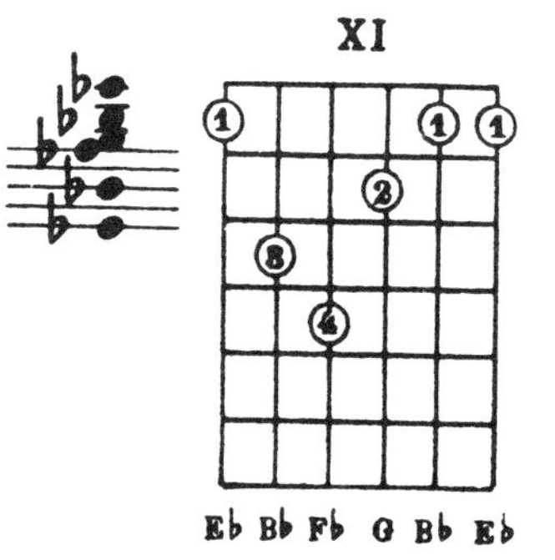

Eb 9 (+5)
Eb-G-B-Db-F

Eb 9 (-5)
Eb-G-Bbb-Db-F

Eb 9 (+5)
Eb 9 (-5)
___
Eb maj. 7
(add 9)
Eb 11
→
Eb aug. 11
Eb 13

Eb maj. 7 (add 9)
Eb-G-Bb-D-F

Eb 11
Eb-G-Bb-Db-F-Ab

Eb aug. 11
Eb-G-Bb-Db-F-A

Eb 13
Eb-G-Bb-Db-F-C

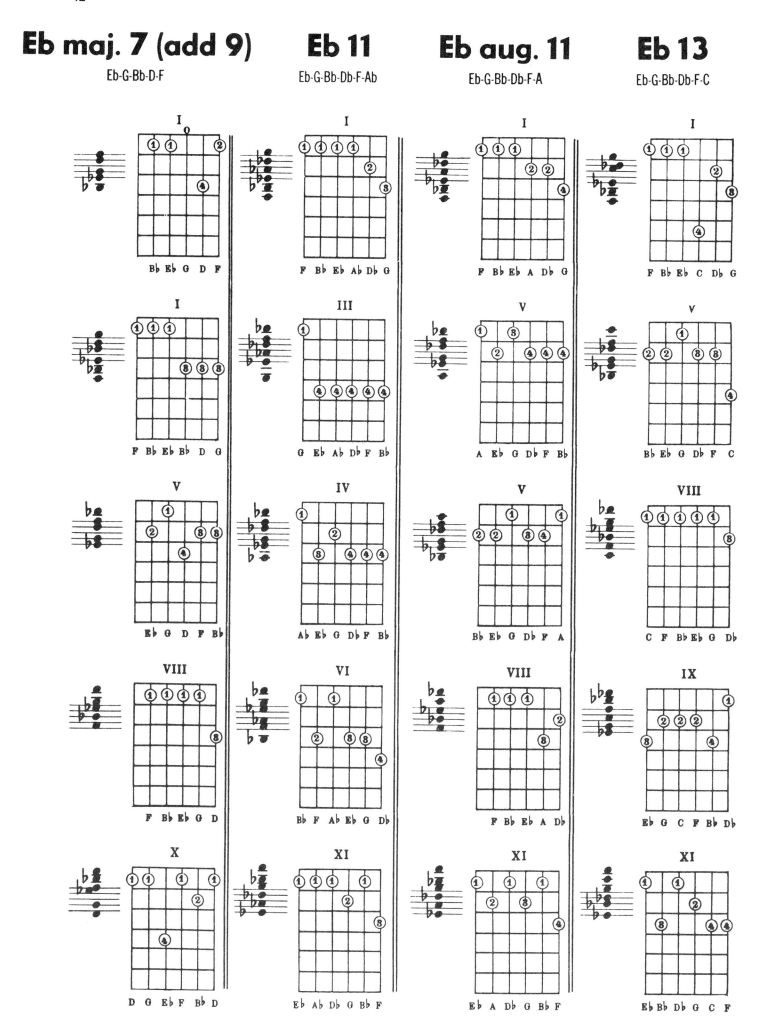

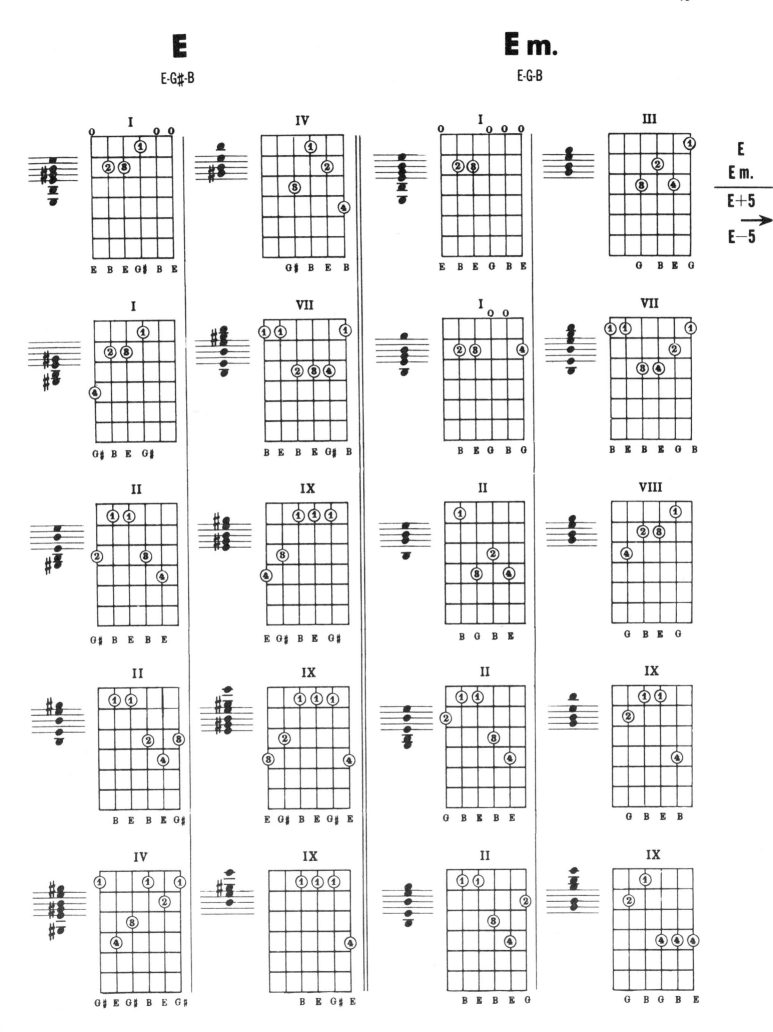

44

E+5
E-G#-B#

E-5
E-G#-Bb

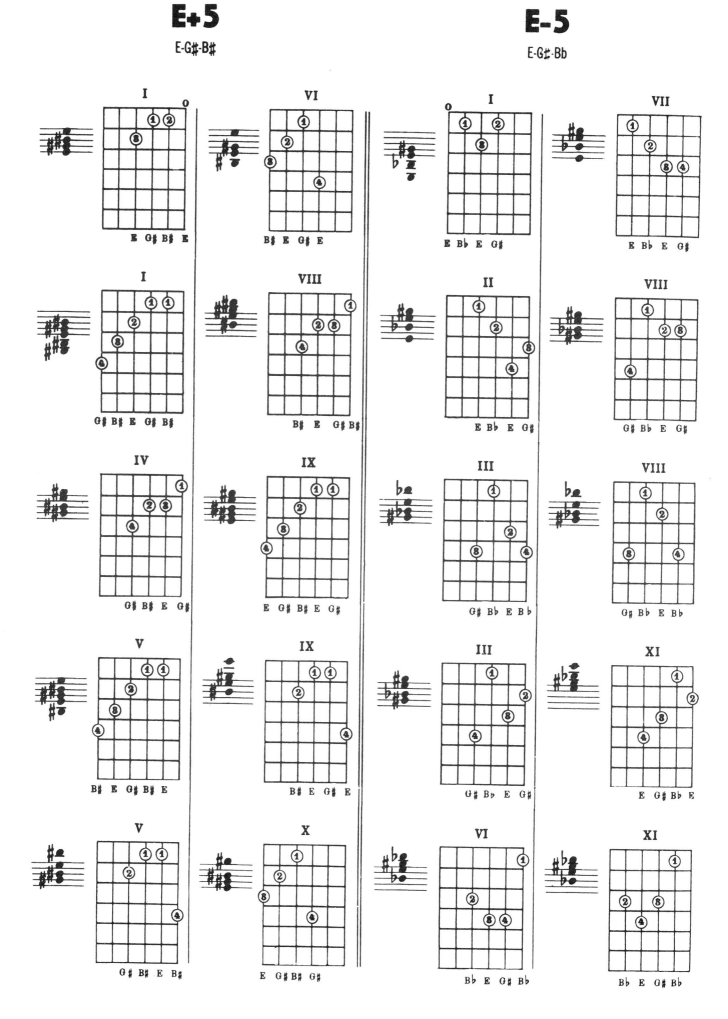

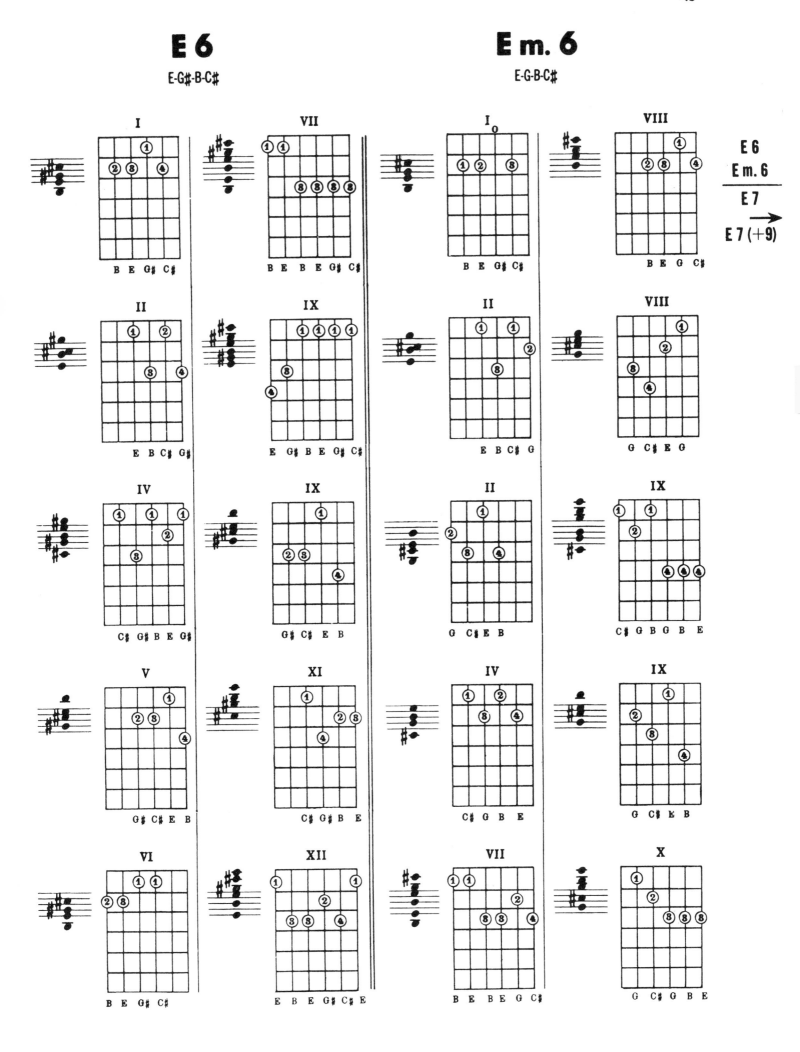

E 7

E-G#-B-D

E 7 (+9)

E-G#-B-D-Fx

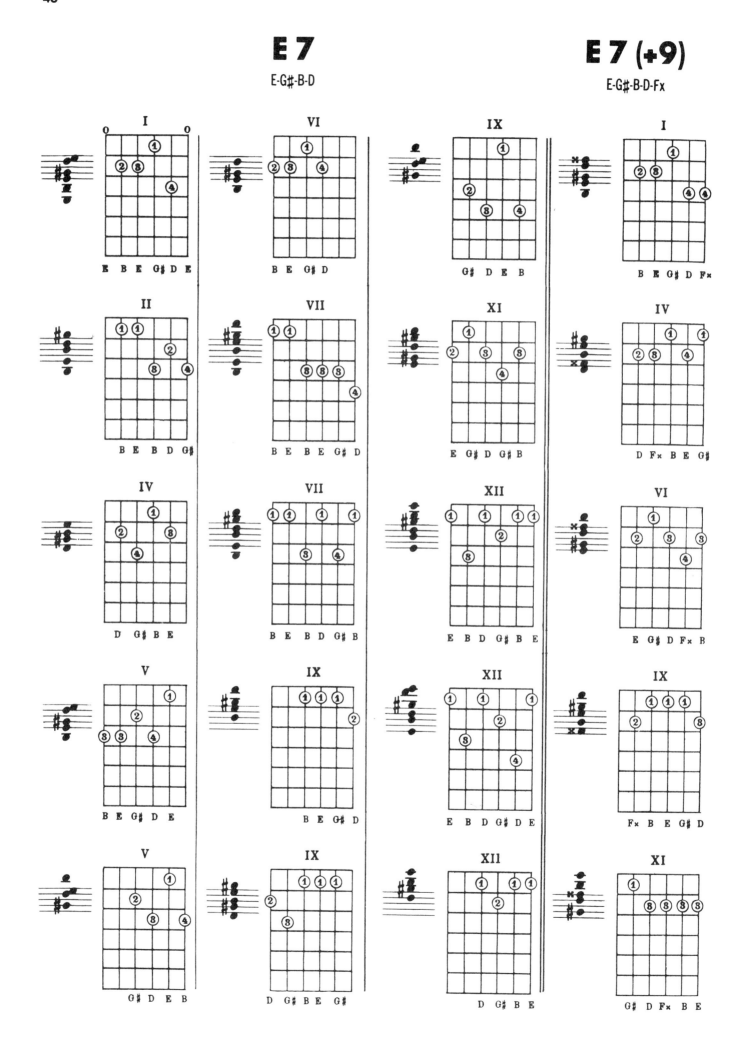

E m. 7

E-G-B-D

E 13 (-9)

E-G♯-B-D-F-C♯

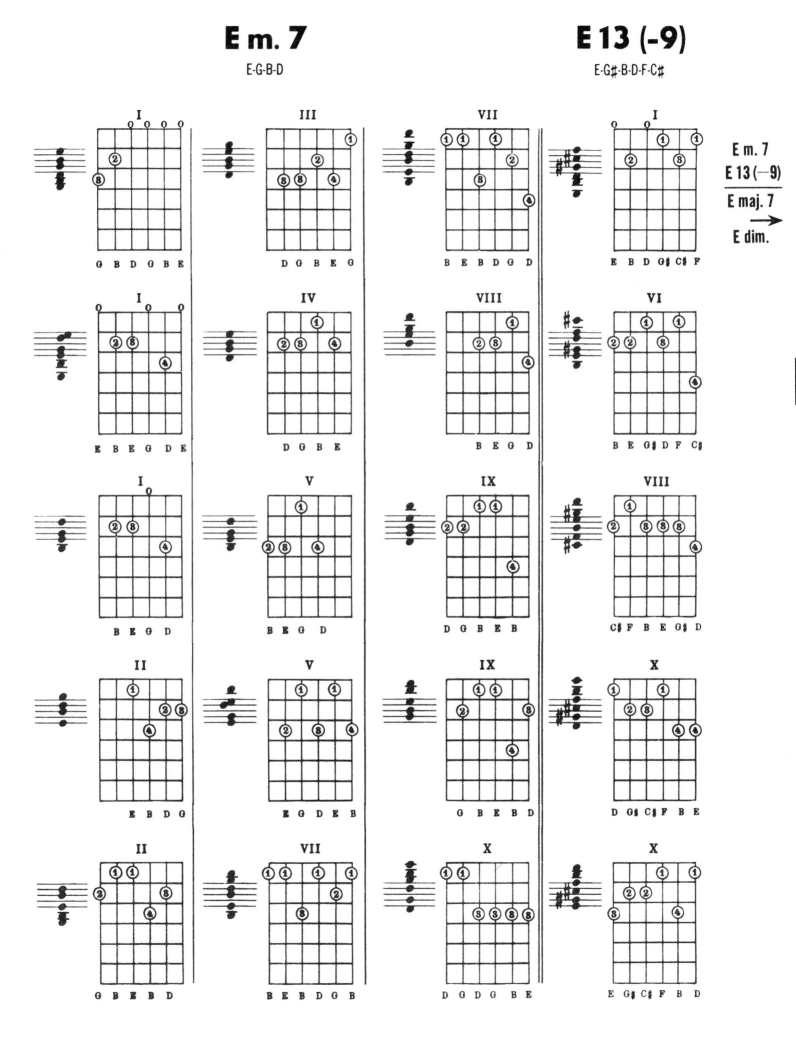

E m. 7
E 13 (—9)
—————
E maj. 7
→
E dim.

48

E maj. 7

E-G#-B-D#

E dim.

E-G-Bb-Db

E B D# G# B E

B E G# D#

B D# G# E

B E B D# G# B

B E G# D# G#

G# B E G# D#

B E B D# G#

D# G# E G# B D#

G# E G# B D# G#

D# G# B E

E Bb Db G

G Db G Bb E G

Db G Bb E

G Db E Bb

Bb E Bb Db G Bb

E Bb Db G

Bb E G Db

Db G D E Bb Db

G Db E Bb

Db G Bb E

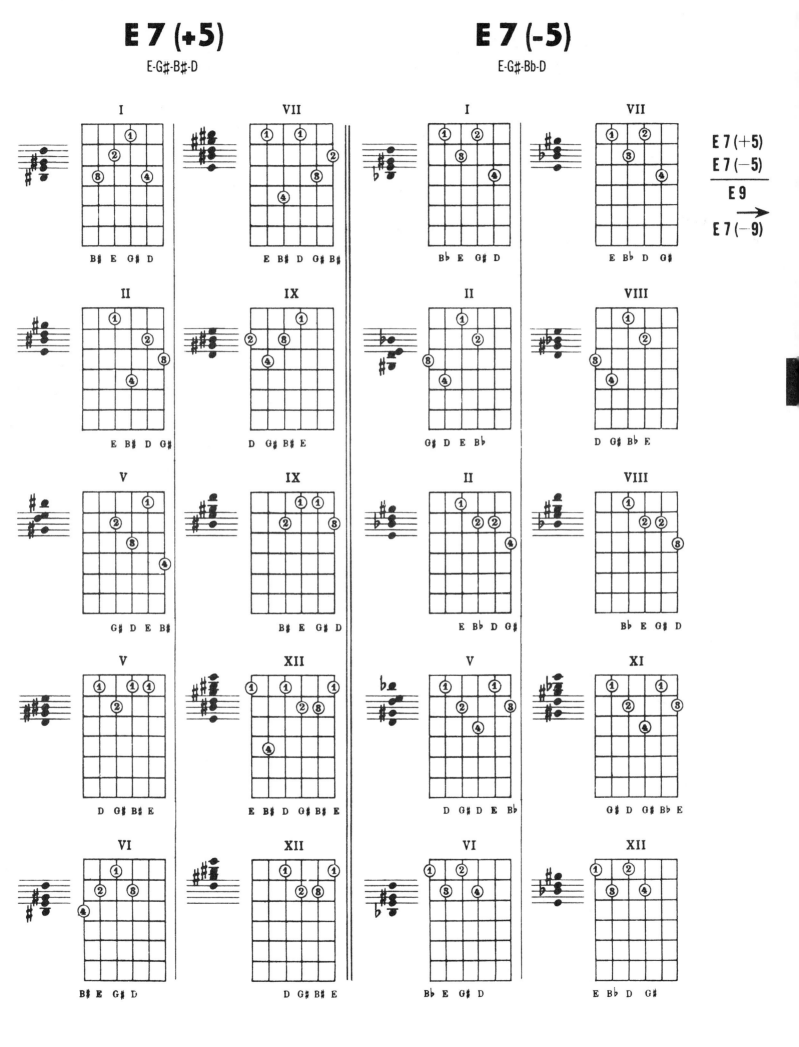

E 9
E-G#-B-D-F#

E 7 (-9)
E-G#-B-D-F

E 9 (+5)
E-G♯-B♯-D-F♯

E 9 (−5)
E-G♯-Bb-D-F♯

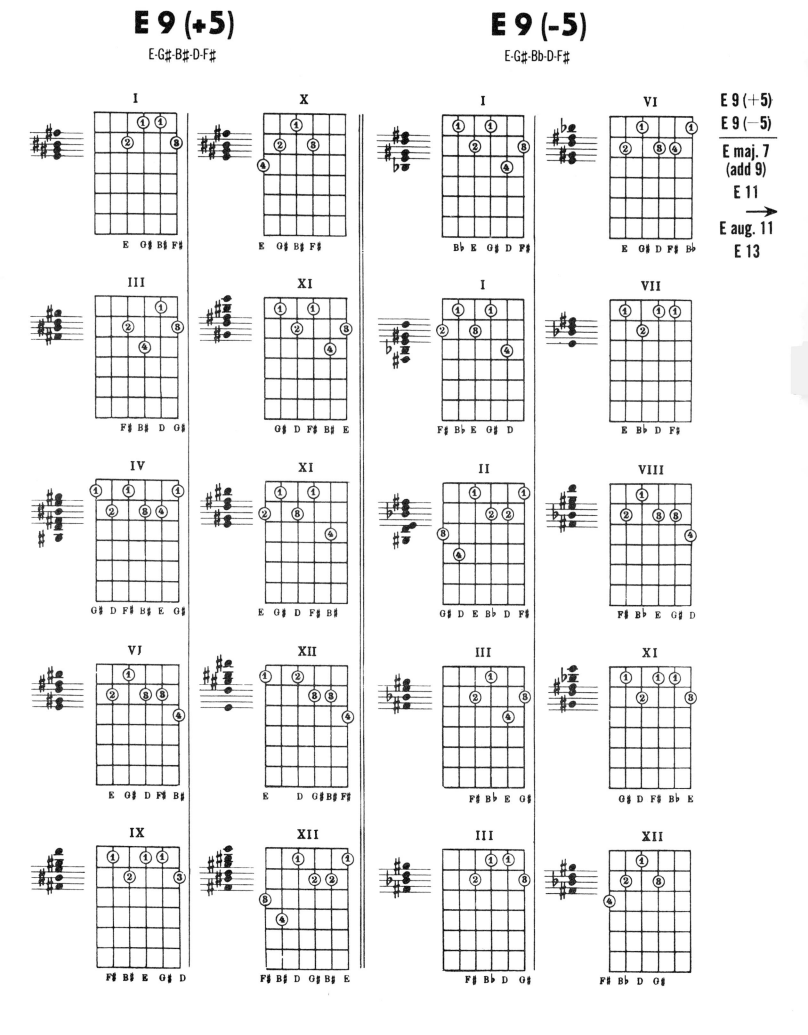

E 9 (+5)
E 9 (−5)
E maj. 7
(add 9)
E 11
→
E aug. 11
E 13

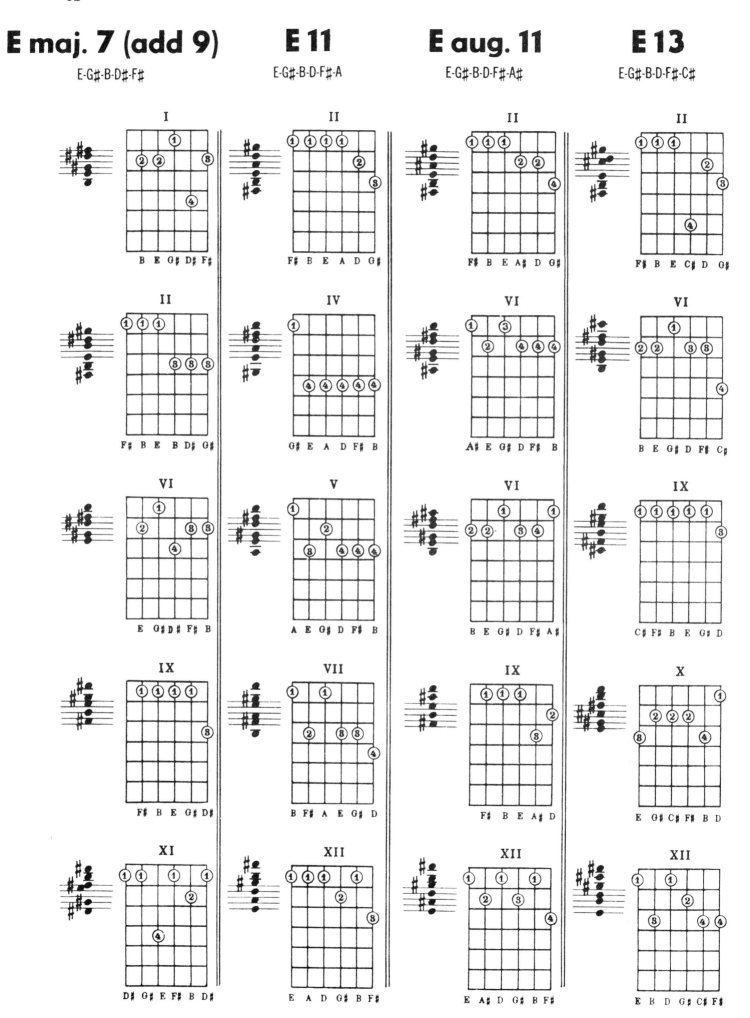

F

F-A-C

F m.

F-Ab-C

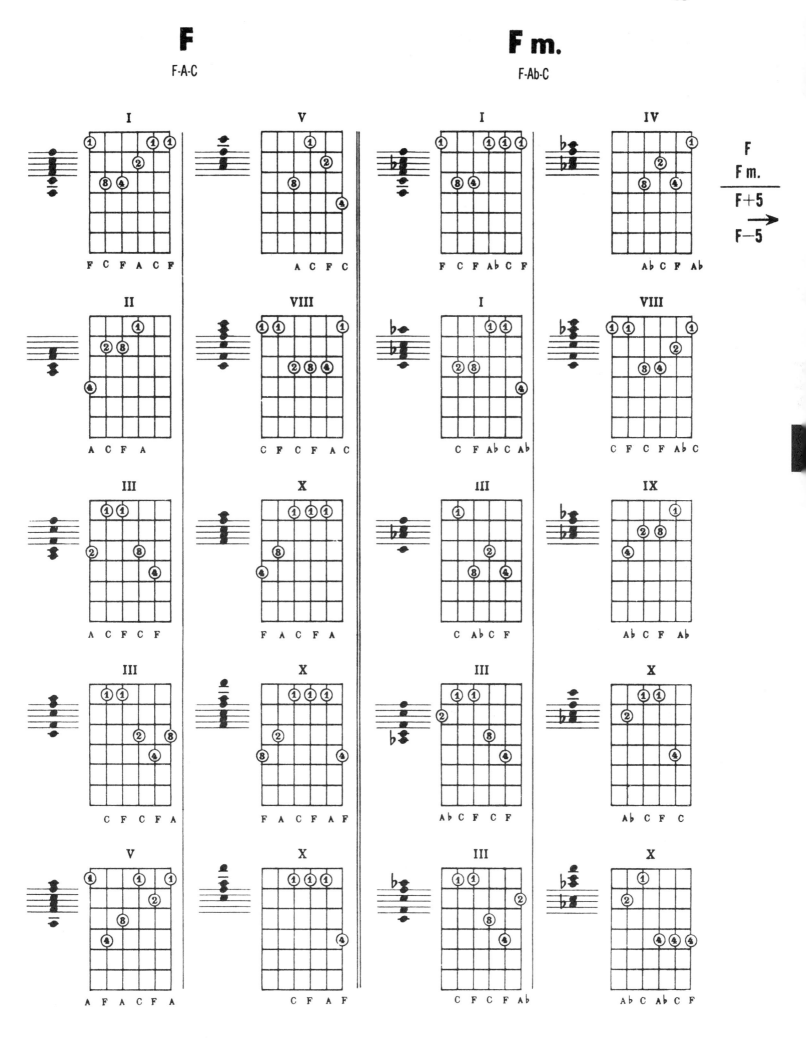

F
F m.
————
F+5
⟶
F—5

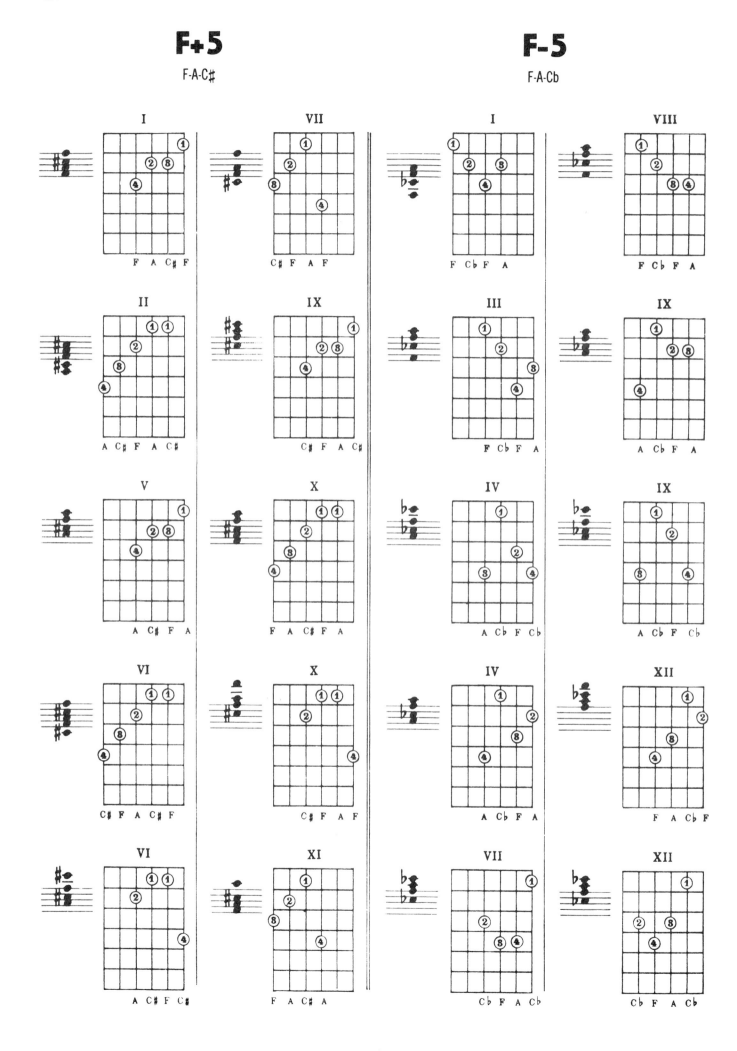

F 6
F-A-C-D

F m. 6
F-Ab-C-D

F 6
Fm. 6
___
F 7
___
F 7 (+9)

F 7

F-A-C-Eb

F 7 (+9)

F-A-C-Eb-G♯

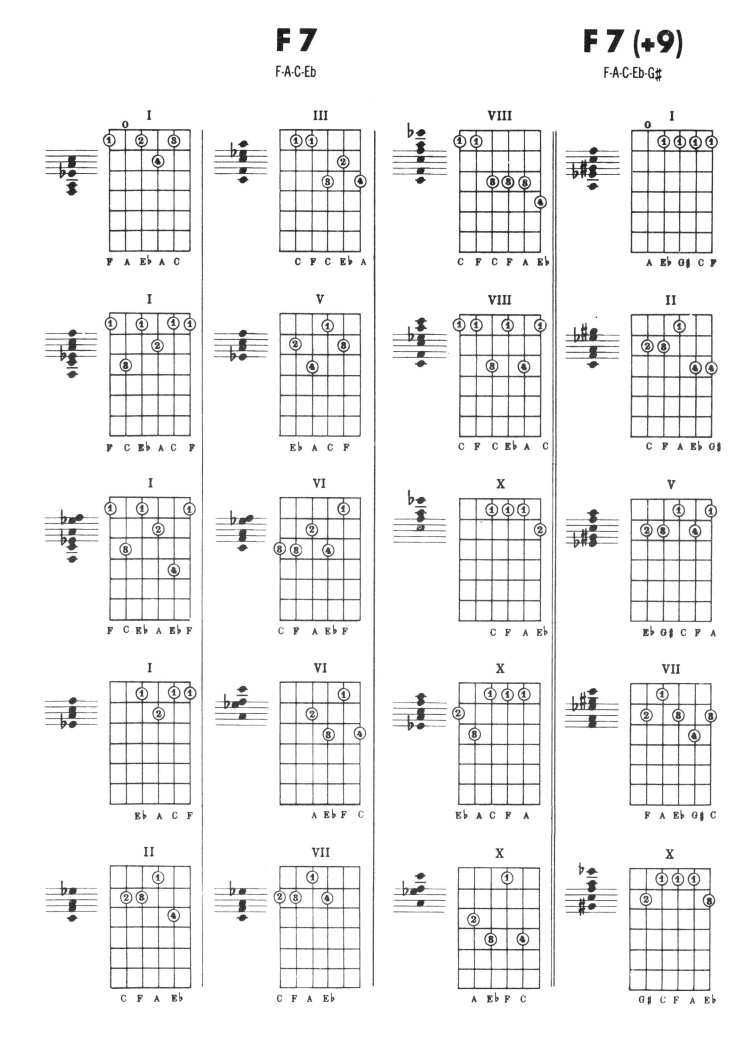

F m. 7

F-Ab-C-Eb

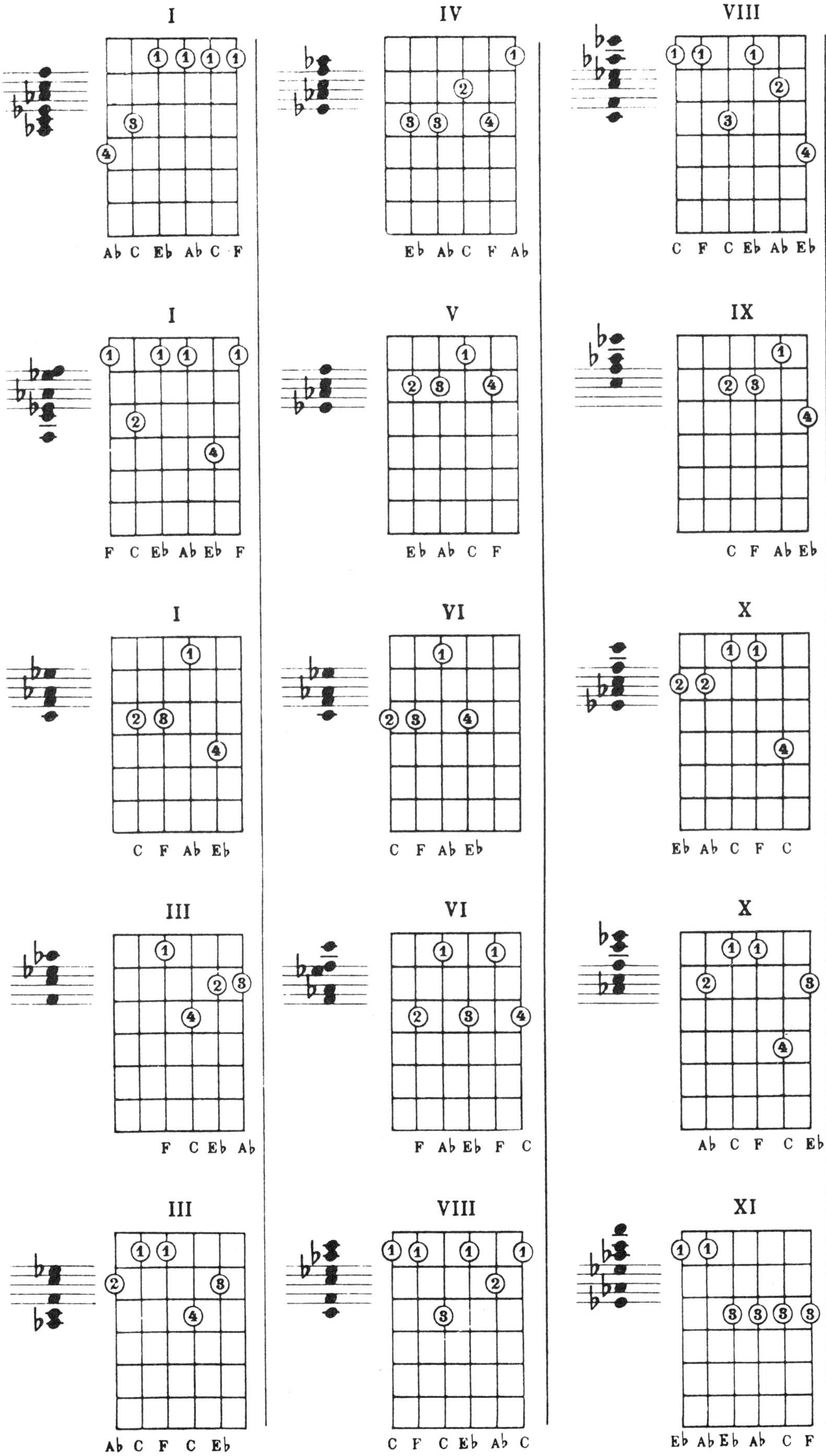

F 13 (-9)

F-A-C-Eb-Gb-D

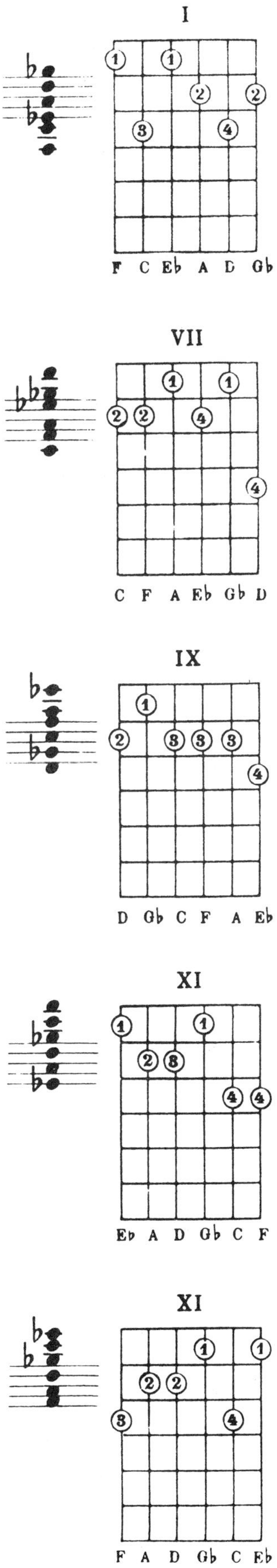

F m. 7
F 13 (-9)
F maj. 7
→
F dim.

F maj. 7
F-A-C-E

F dim.
F-Ab-Cb-Ebb

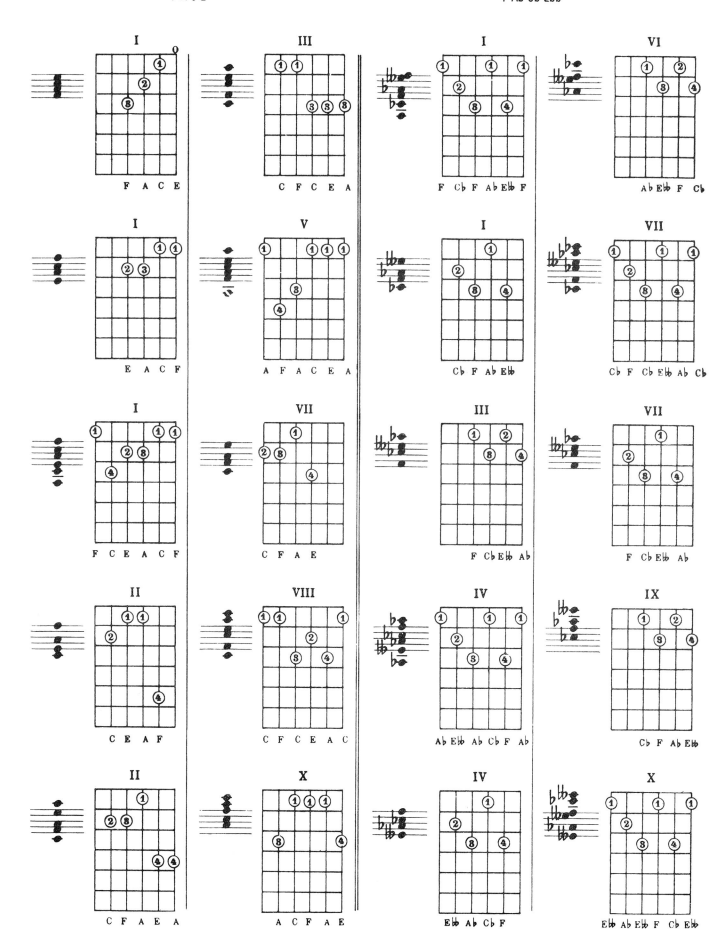

F 7 (+5)
F-A-C#-Eb

F 7 (-5)
F-A-Cb-Eb

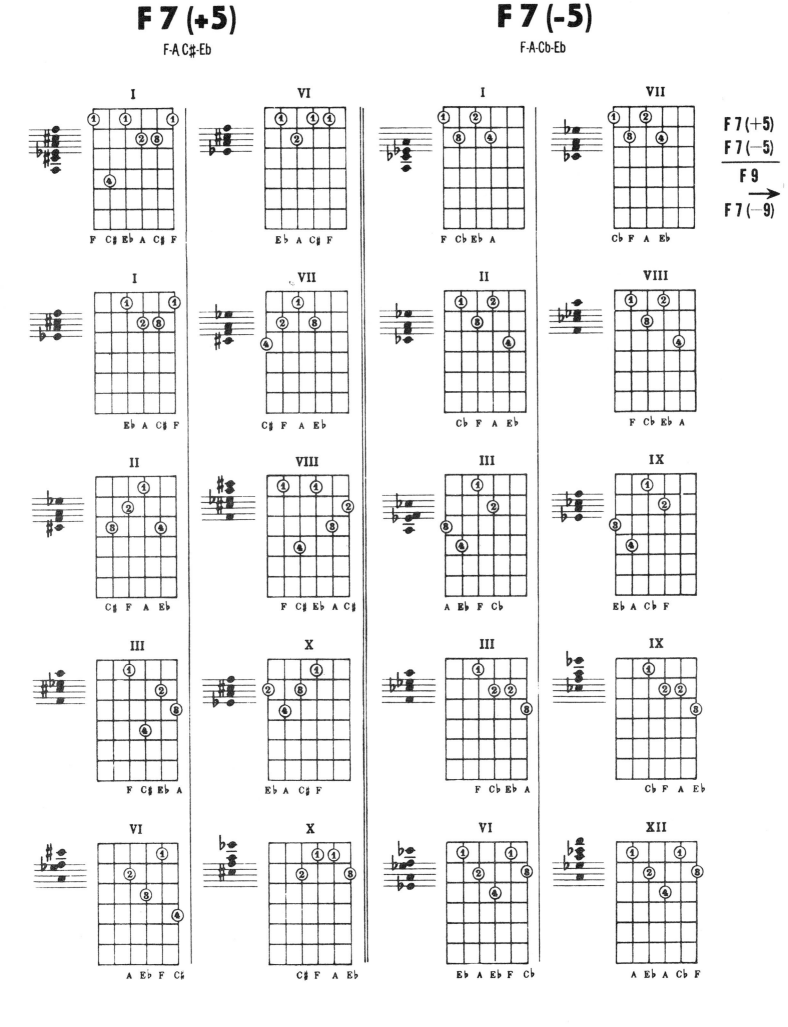

F 7 (+5)
F 7 (-5)
─────
F 9
→
F 7 (-9)

F 9
F-A-C-Eb-G

F 7 (-9)
F-A-C-Eb-Gb

I

F C Eb A C G

V

A Eb G C F A

I

F C Eb A C Gb

VIII

Gb C Eb A C

I

G C Eb A C F

VII

C F A Eb G C

I

F C Gb A C F

IX

Gb C F A Eb

II

C F A Eb G

X

G C F A Eb

II

C F A Eb Gb

X

C Gb A Eb

III

G C F C Eb A

X

F G C G A Eb

IV

Eb Gb C F A

XI

F A Gb C Eb

IV

G C Eb A

XII

A Eb G C F

VII

F A Eb Gb C

XI

A Eb Gb C F

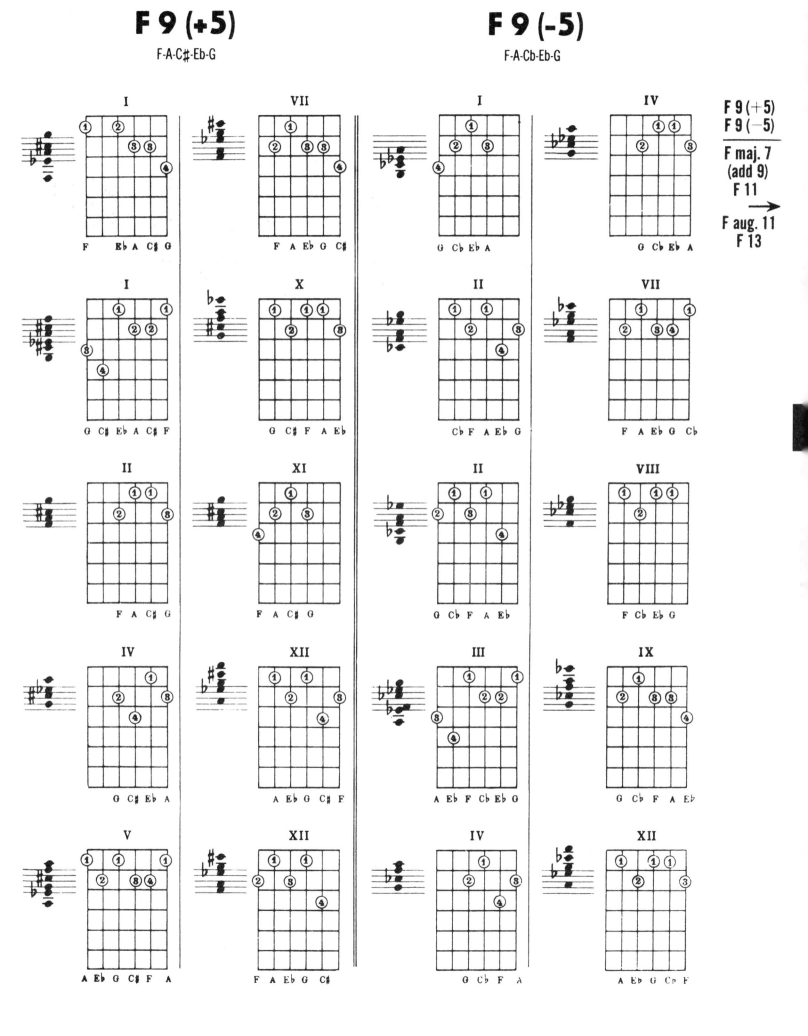

F maj. 7 (add 9)
F-A-C-E-G

F 11
F-A-C-Eb-G-Bb

F aug. 11
F-A-C-Eb-G-B

F 13
F-A-C-Eb-G-D

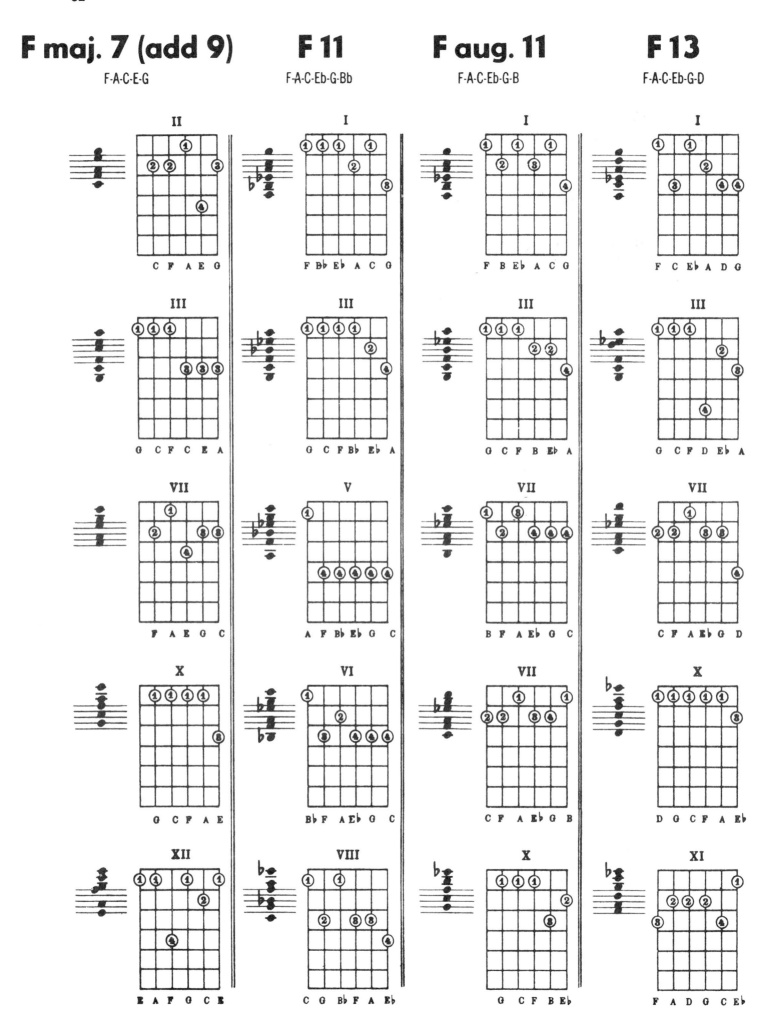

Gb or F#

Gb-Bb-Db   F#-A#-C#

Gb m. or F# m.

Gb-Bbb-Db   F#-A-C#

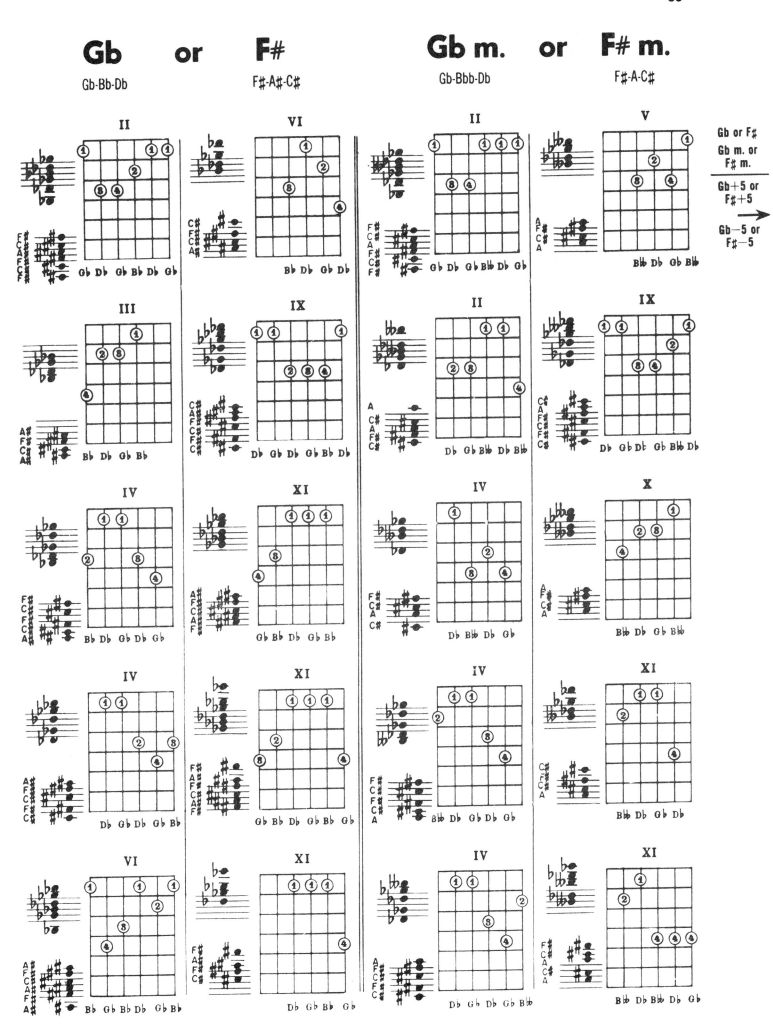

Gb or F#
Gb m. or F# m.
Gb+5 or F#+5
Gb—5 or F#—5
→

Gb+5 or F#+5

Gb-Bb-D   F#-A#-Cx

Gb-5 or F#-5

Gb-Bb-Dbb   F#-A#-C

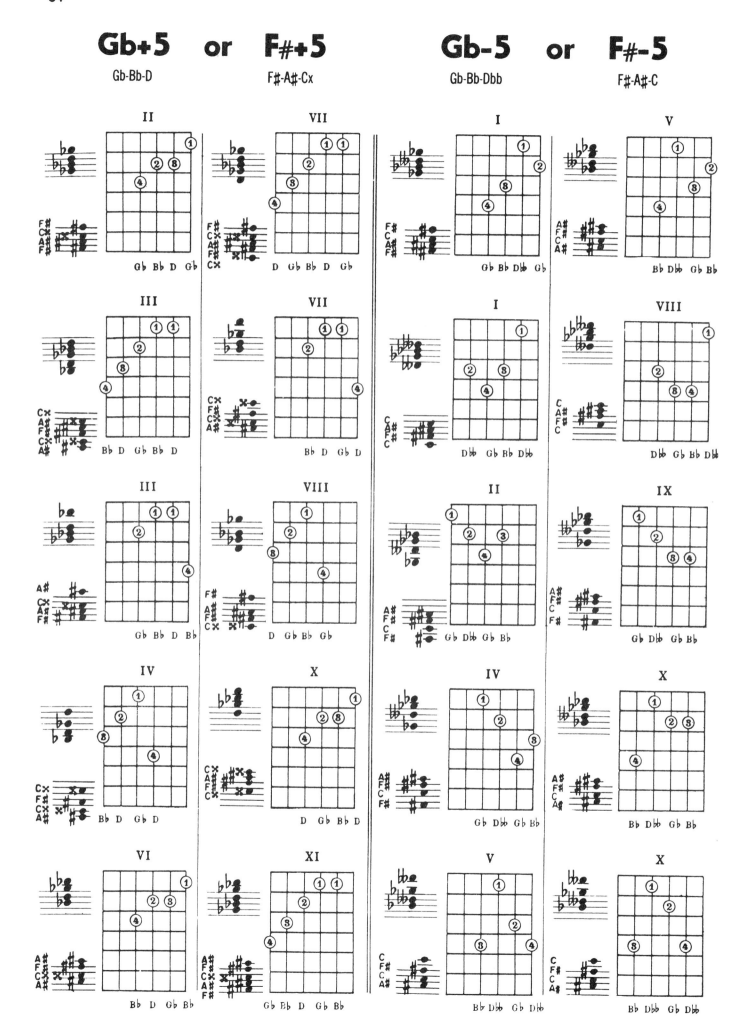

Gb 6 or F# 6

Gb-Bb-Db-Eb

F#-A#-C#-D#

Gb m. 6 or F# m. 6

Gb-Bbb-Db-Eb

F#-A-C#-D#

Gb 6 or
F# 6

Gb m. 6 or
F# m. 6

Gb 7 or
F# 7

→

Gb 7 (+9) or
F# 7 (+9)

Gb 7　or　F# 7　　Gb 7 (+9)

Gb-Bb-Db-Fb　　F#-A#-C#-E　　Gb-Bb-Db-Fb-A

or

F# 7 (+9)

F#-A#-C#-E-Gx

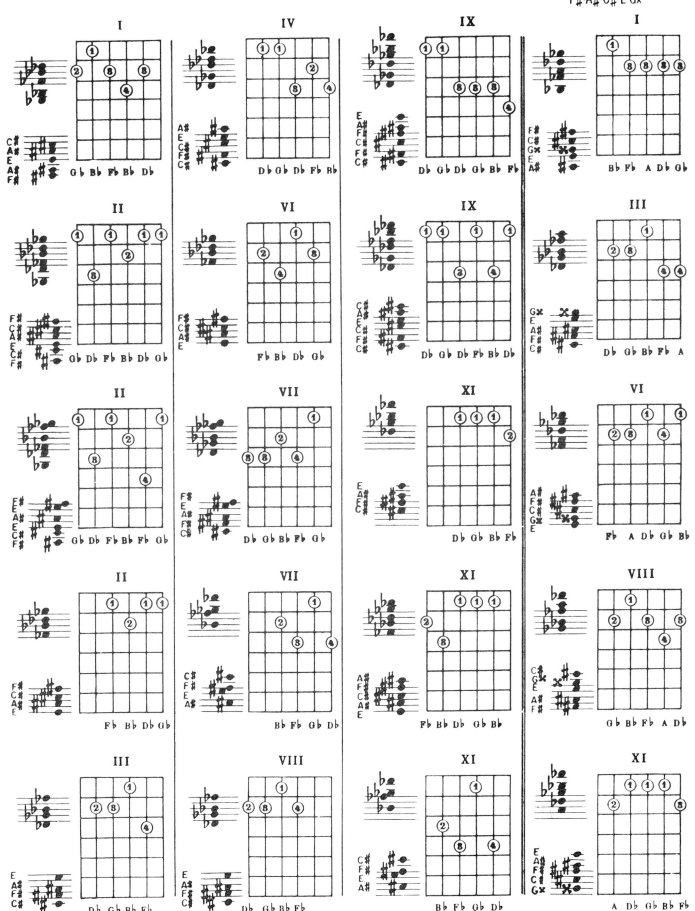

Gb m. 7 or F# m. 7

Gb-Bbb-Db-Fb   F#-A-C#-E

Gb 13 (-9) ⁶⁷

Gb-Bb-Db-Fb-Abb-Eb

F# 13 (-9) or

F#-A#-C#-E-G-D#

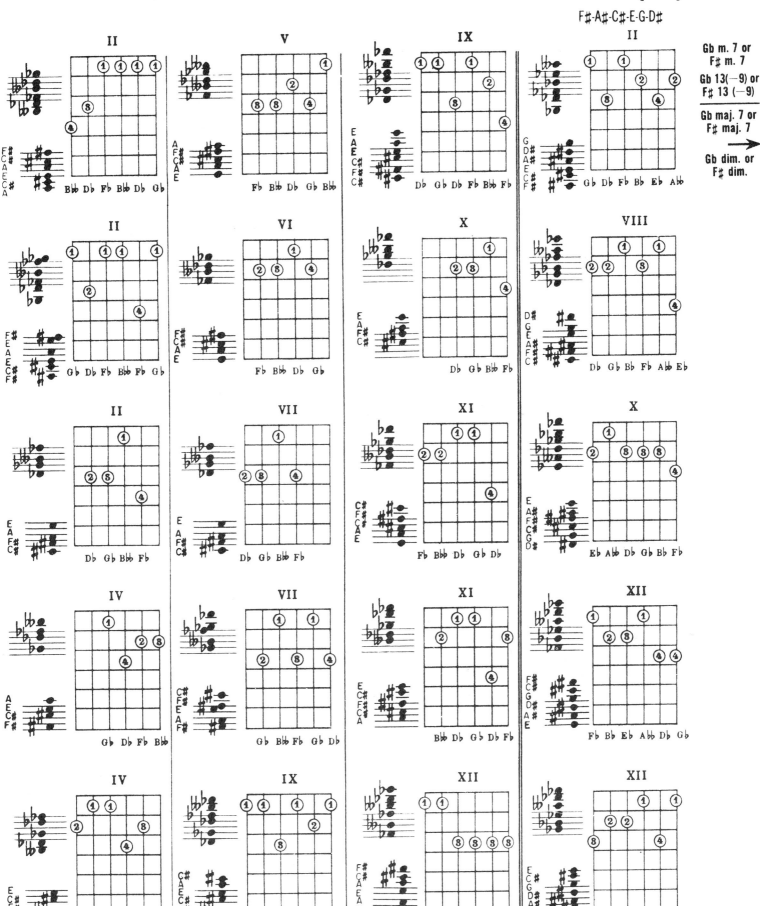

Gb m. 7 or
F# m. 7

Gb 13(—9) or
F# 13 (—9)

Gb maj. 7 or
F# maj. 7
→
Gb dim. or
F# dim.

Gb maj. 7 or F# maj. 7

Gb-Bb-Db-F   F#-A#-C#-E#

Gb dim. or F# dim.

Gb-Bbb-Dbb-Fbb   F#-A-C-Eb

Gb 7 (+5) or F# 7 (+5)

Gb-Bb-D-Fb   F#-A#-Cx-E

Gb 7 (-5) or F# 7 (-5)

Gb-Bb-Dbb-Fb   F#-A#-C-E

Gb 7 (+5) or
F# 7 (+5)

Gb 7 (−5) or
F# 7 (−5)
_____
Gb 9 or
F# 9
→
Gb 7 (−9) or
F# 7 (−9)

Gb 9 or F# 9

Gb-Bb-Db-Fb-Ab   F#-A#-C#-E-G#

Gb 7 (-9) or F# 7 (-9)

Gb-Bb-Db-Fb-Abb   F#-A#-C#-E-G

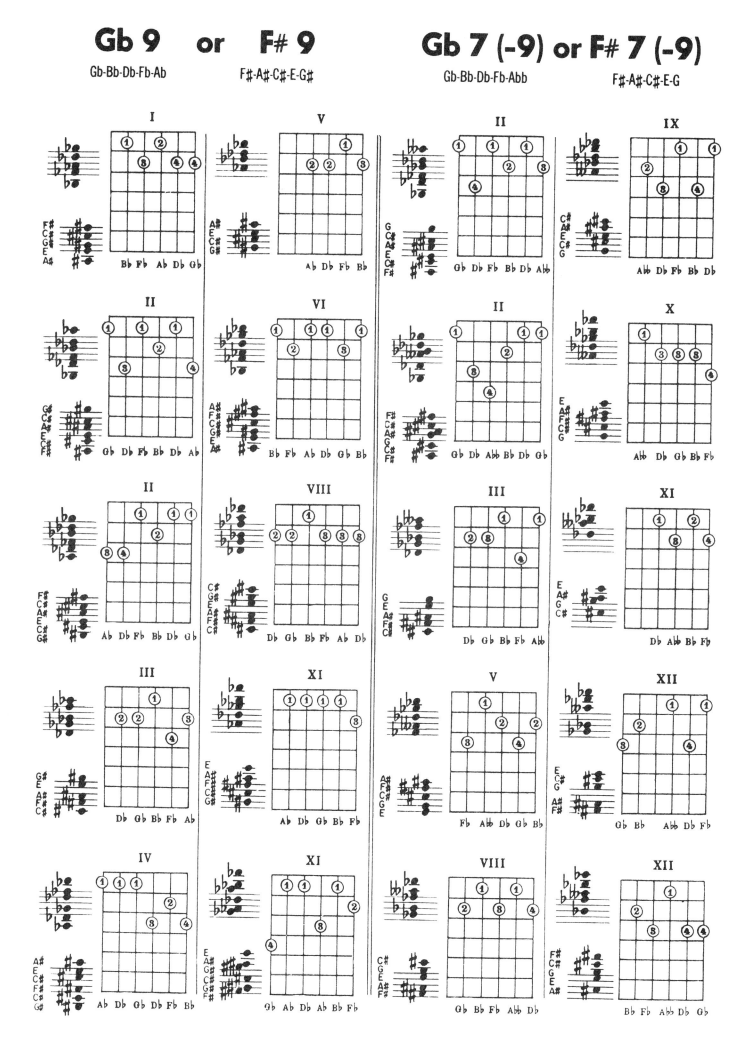

Gb 9 (+5) or F# 9 (+5)

Gb-Bb-D-Fb-Ab   F#-A#-Cx-E-G#

Gb 9 (−5) or F# 9 (−5)

Gb-Bb-Dbb-Fb-Ab   F#-A#-C-E-G#

Gb 9 (+5) or
F# 9 (+5)
Gb 9 (−5) or
F# 9 (−5)
Gb maj. 7 (add 9) or
F# maj. 7 (add 9)
Gb 11 or
F# 11
Gb aug. 11 or
F# aug. 11
Gb 13 or
F# 13
→

Gb maj. 7 (add 9)
Gb-Bb-Db-F-Ab

or

F# maj. 7 (add 9)
F#-A#-C#-E#-G#

Gb 11
Gb-Bb-Db-Fb-Ab-Cb

or F# 11
F#-A#-C#-E-G#-B

Gb aug. 11
Gb-Bb-Db-Fb-Ab-C

or F# aug. 11
F#-A#-C#-E-G#-B#

Gb 13
Gb-Bb-Db-Fb-Ab-Eb

or F# 13
F#-A#-C#-E-G#-D#

G

G-B-D

G m.

G-Bb-D

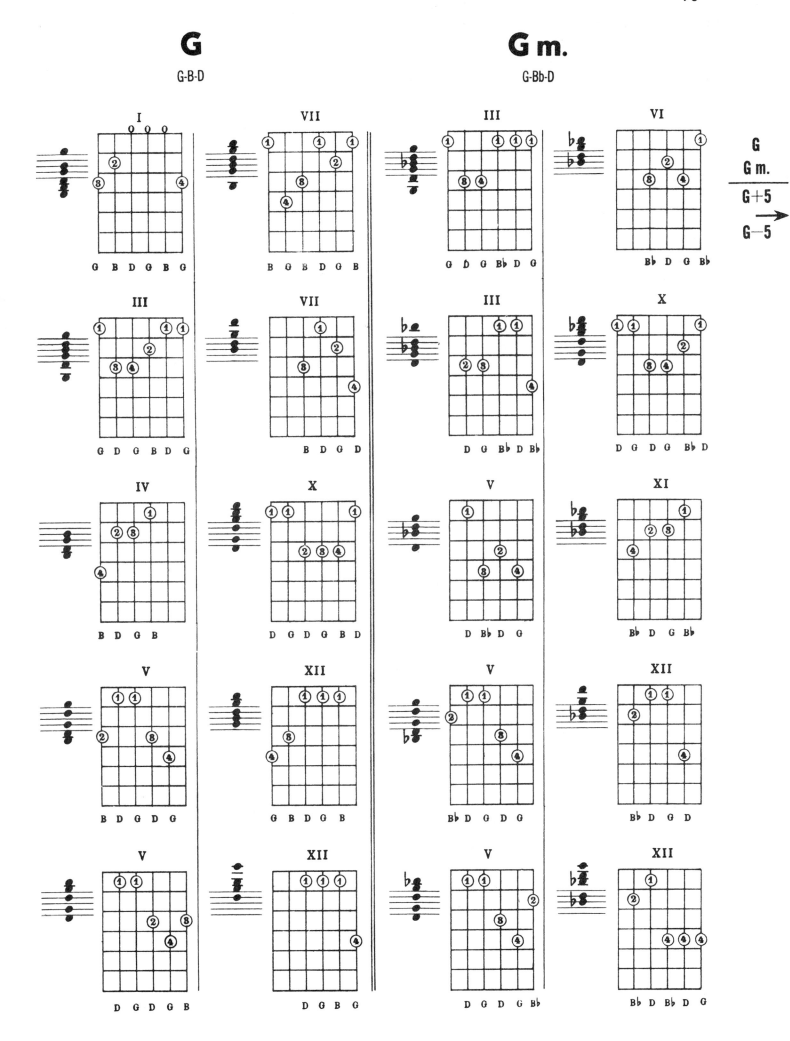

G
G m.
―――
G+5
→
G—5

G+5

G-B-D♯

G-5

G-B-Db

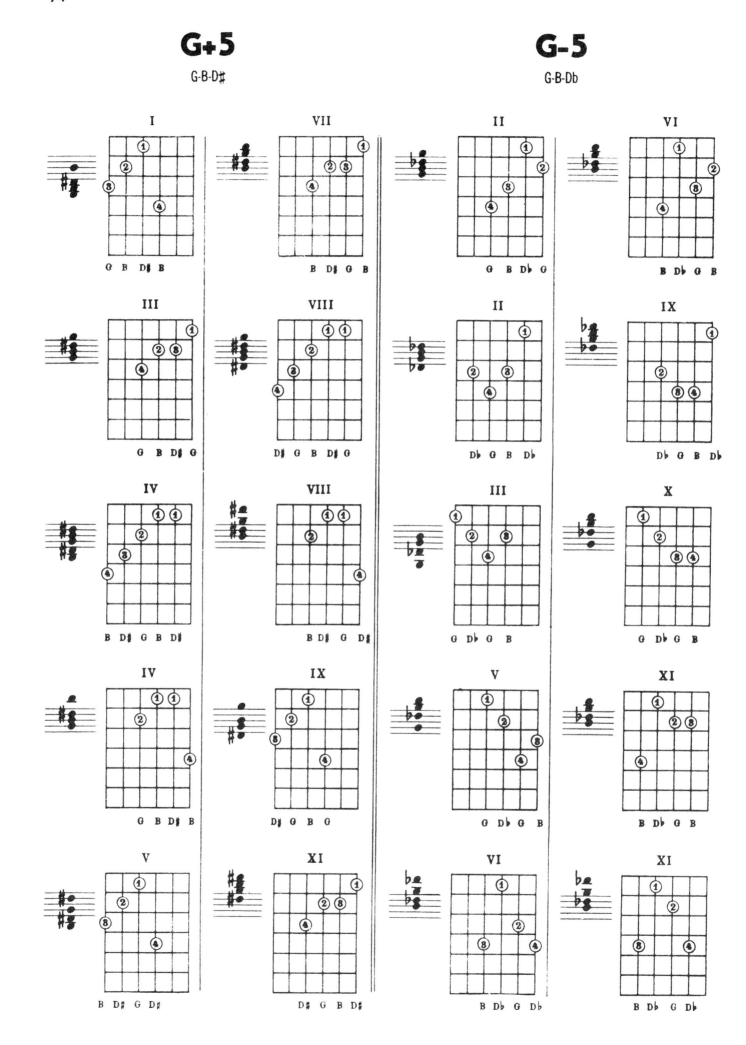

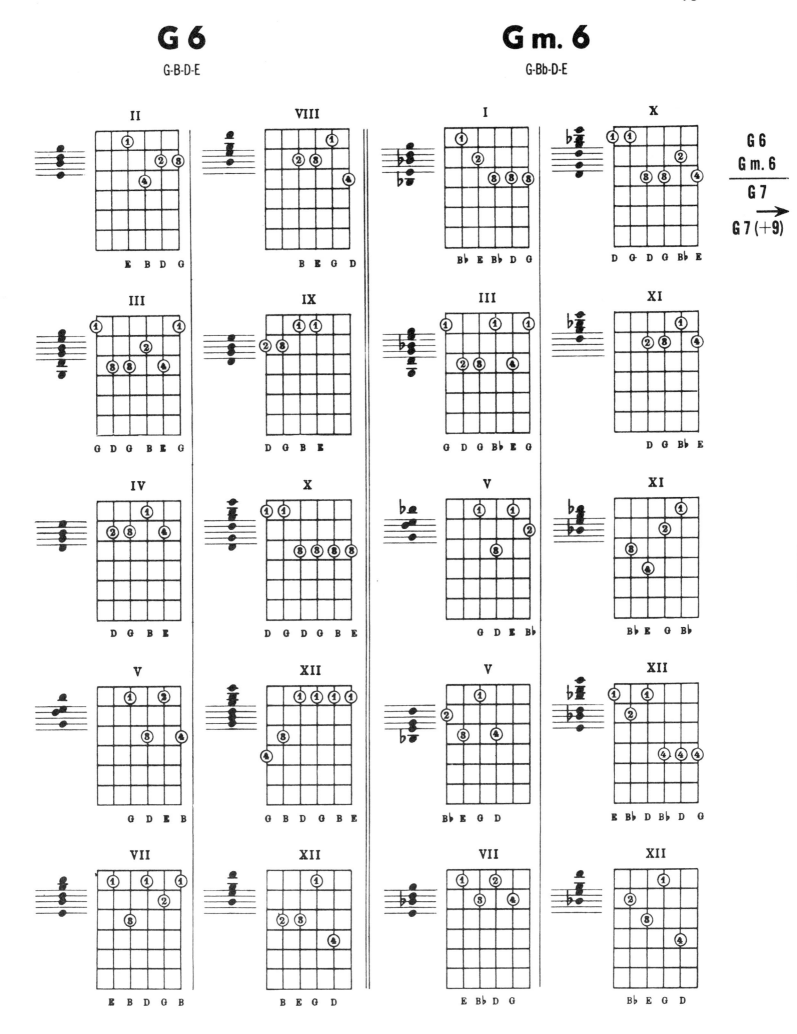

G 7
G-B-D-F

G 7 (+9)
G-B-D-F-A♯

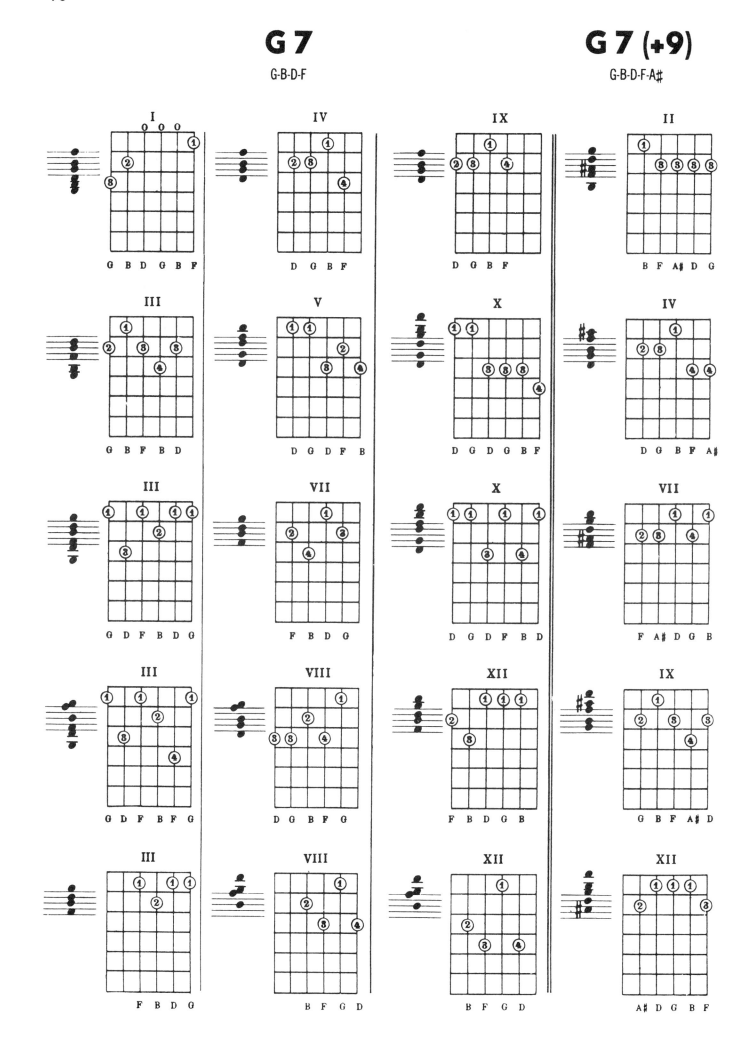

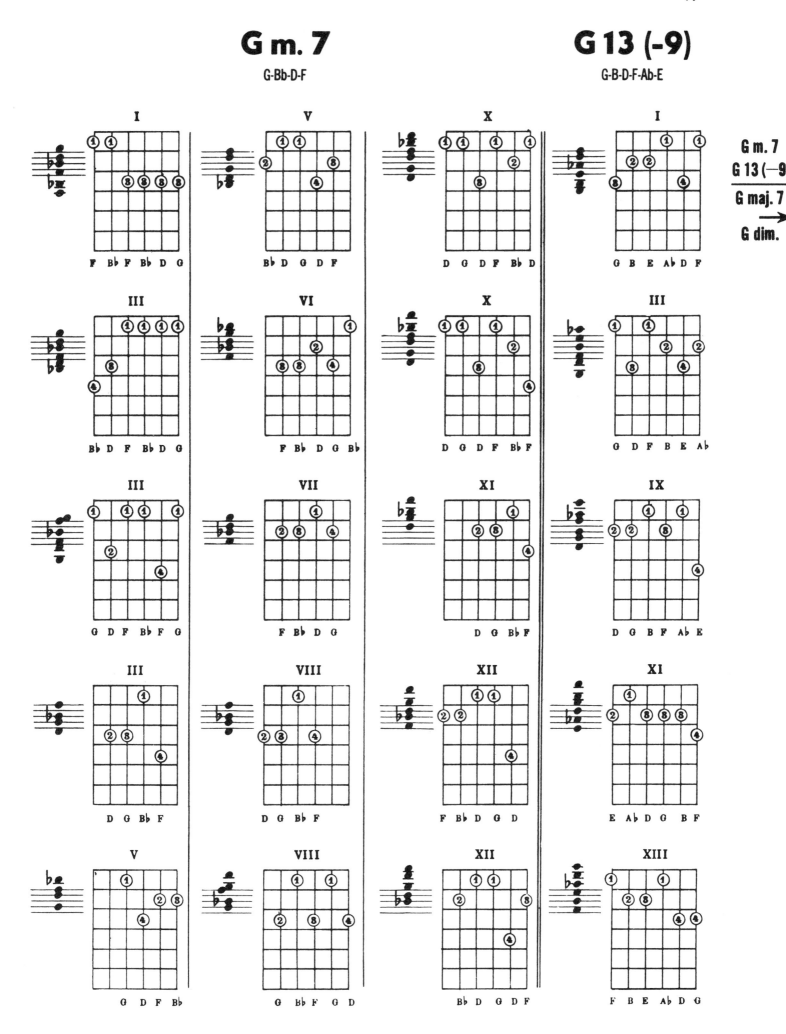

G maj. 7

G-B-D-F#

G dim.

G-Bb-Db-Fb

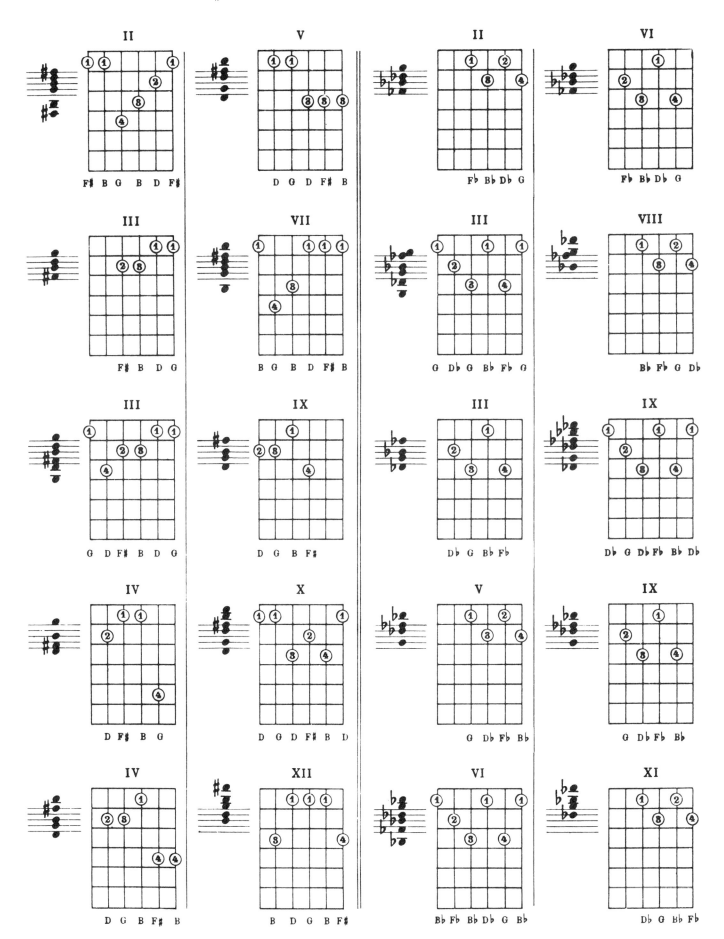

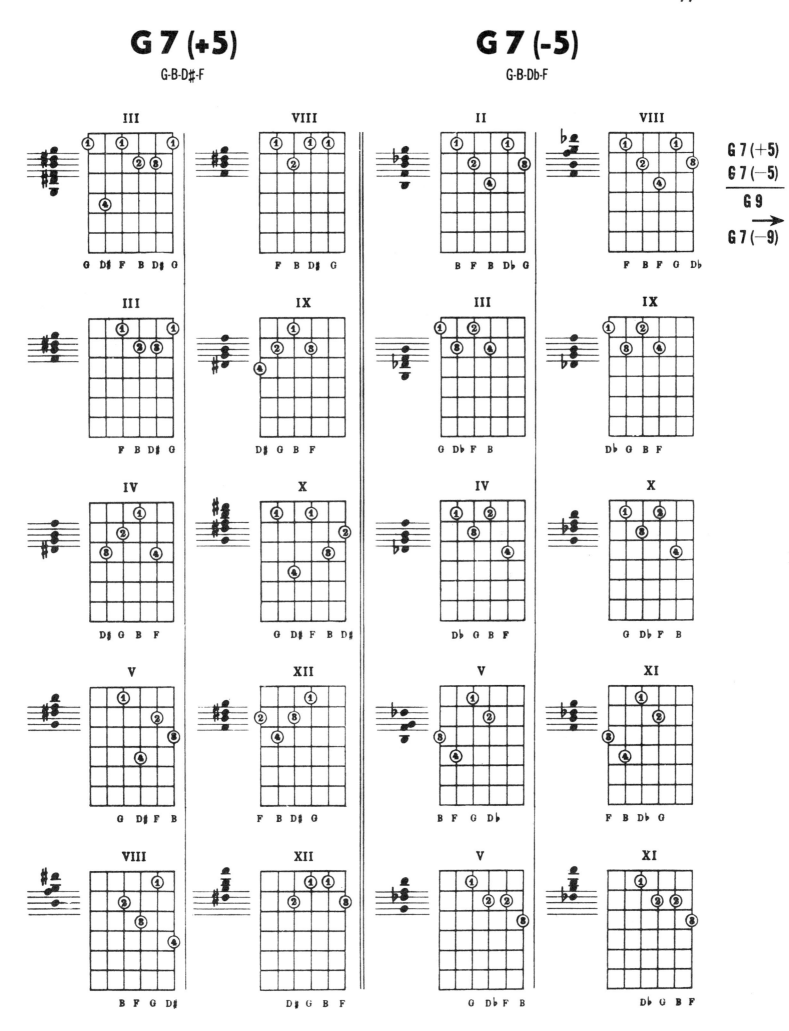

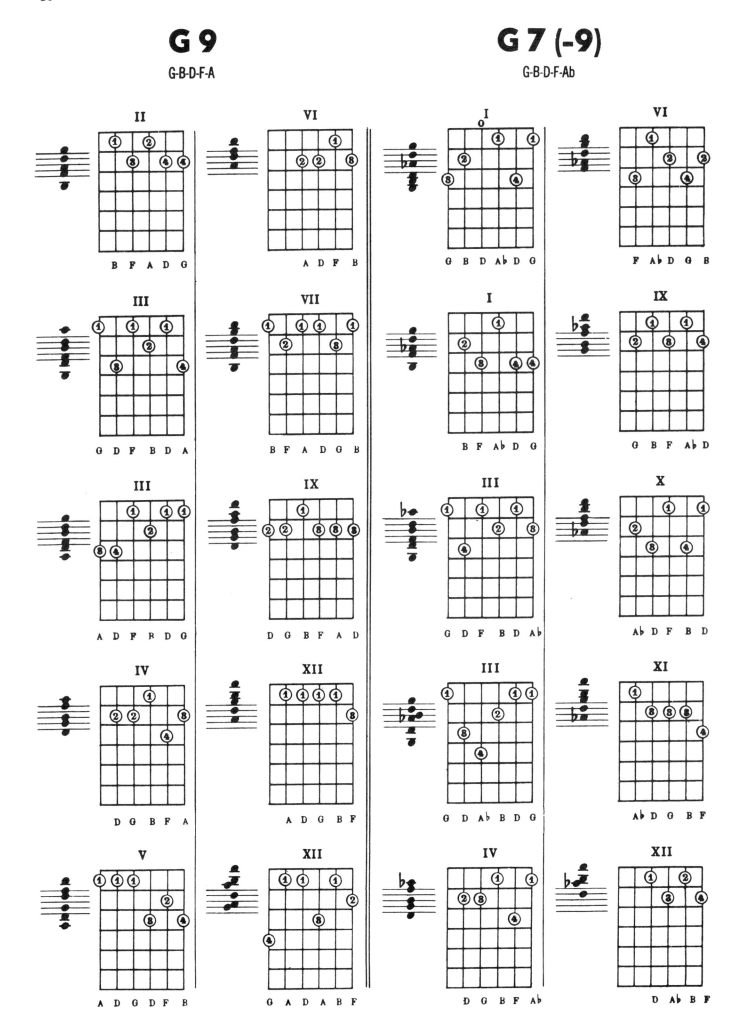

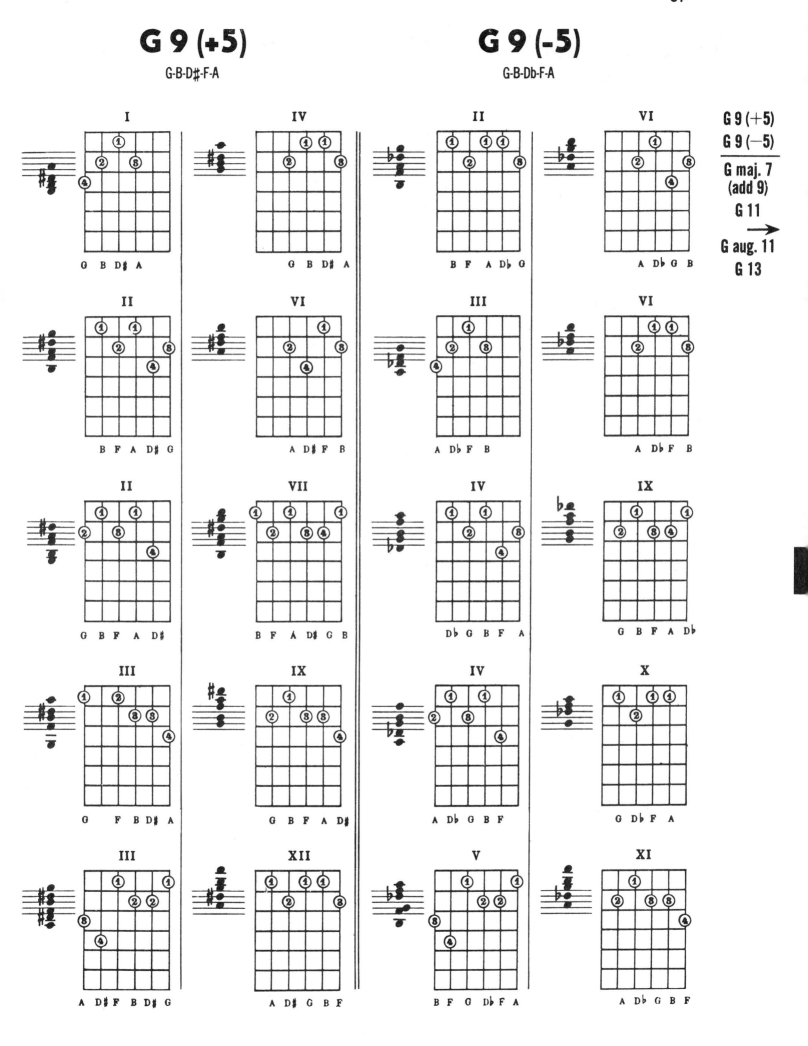

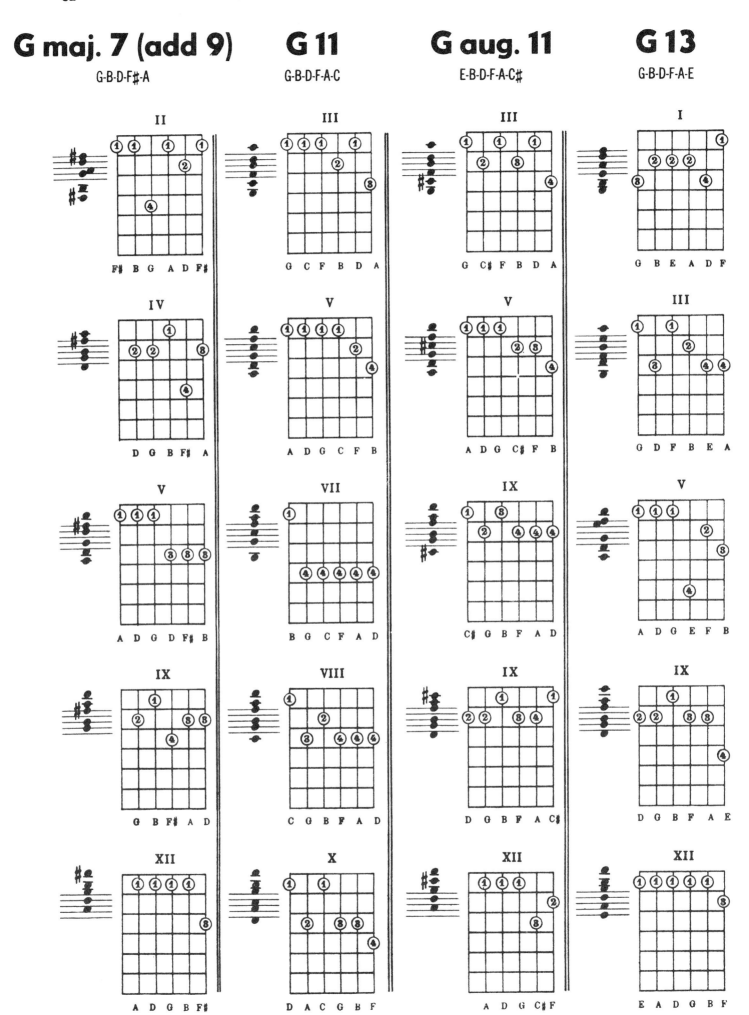

Ab

Ab-C-Eb

Ab m.

Ab-Cb-Eb

I

Ab C Eb Ab C

VI

C Eb Ab Eb Ab

I

Ab C Eb Ab C Ab

VI

Eb Ab Eb Ab C

I

Eb Ab C Ab

VIII

C Ab C Eb Ab C

IV

Ab Eb Ab C Eb Ab

VIII

C Eb Ab Eb

V

C Eb Ab C

XI

Eb Ab Eb Ab C Eb

I

Cb Eb Ab Cb

VI

Cb Eb Ab Eb Ab

I

Cb Eb Cb Eb Ab

VI

Eb Ab Eb Ab Cb

IV

Ab Eb Ab Cb Eb Ab

VII

Cb Eb Ab Cb

IV

Eb Ab Cb Eb Cb

XI

Eb Ab Eb Ab Cb Eb

VI

Eb Cb Eb Ab

XII

Cb Eb Ab Cb

Ab

Ab m.

————

Ab+5

→

Ab−5

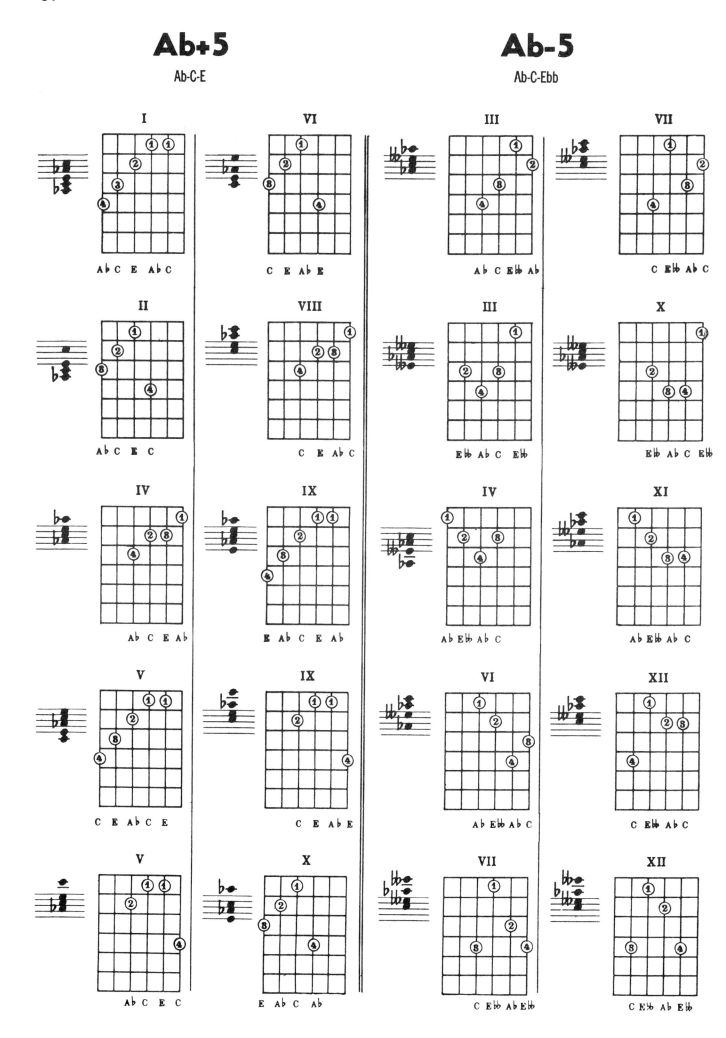

Ab 6

Ab-C-Eb-F

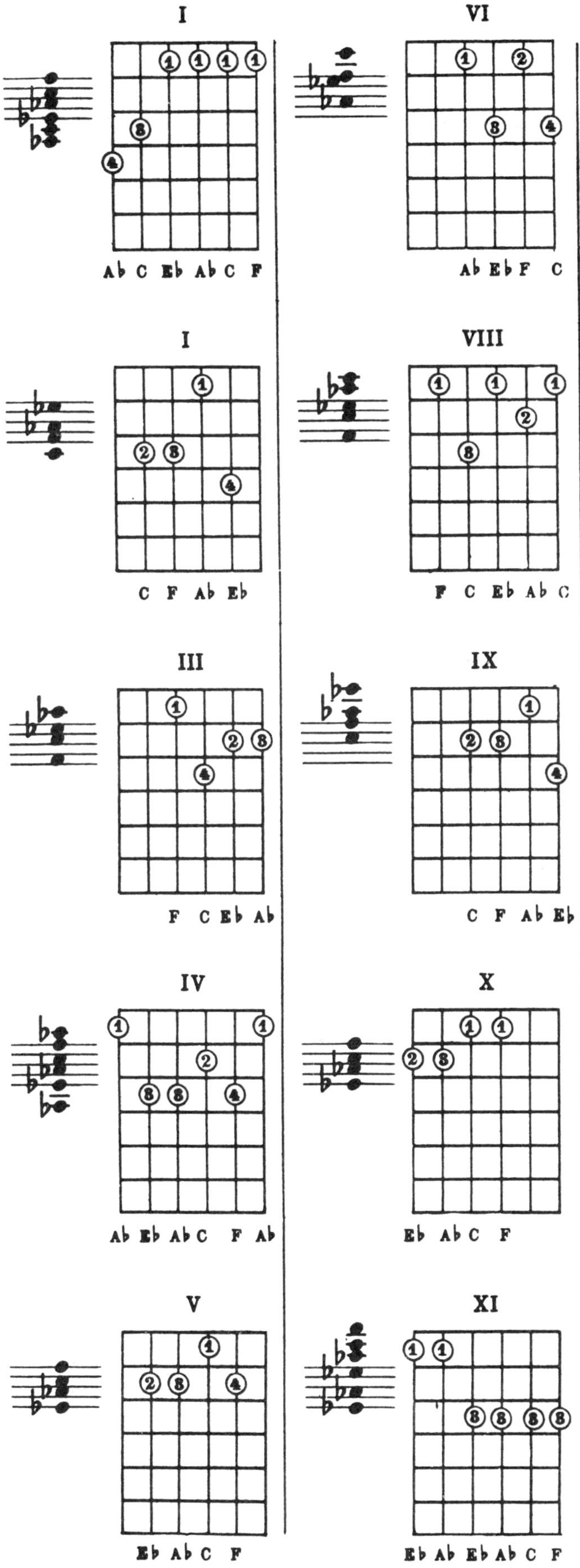

Ab m. 6

Ab-Cb-Eb-F

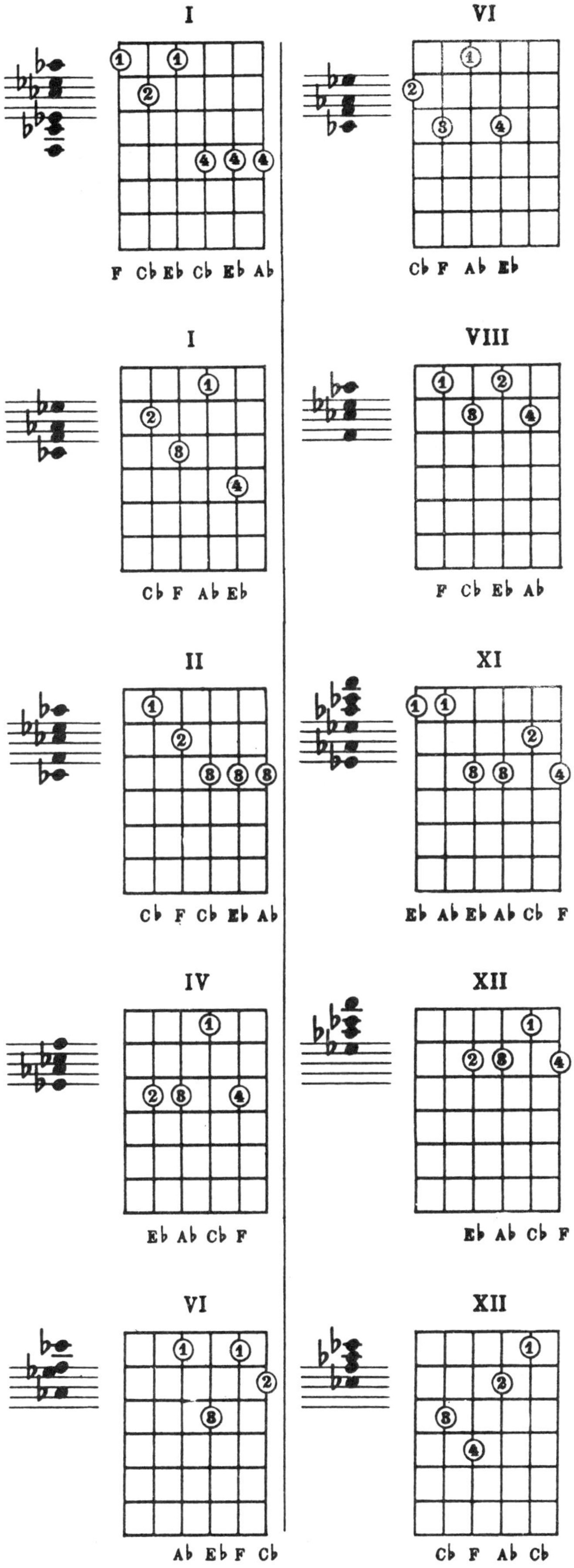

Ab 6
Ab m. 6

Ab 7
→
Ab 7 (+9)

Ab 7

Ab-C-Eb-Gb

Ab 7 (+9)

Ab-C-Eb-Gb-B

I
Eb Ab C Gb

IV
Ab Eb Gb C Gb Ab

IX
Eb Ab C Gb Ab

I
B Eb Ab C Gb

I
Gb C Eb Ab C

IV
Gb C Eb Ab

IX
C Gb Ab Eb

III
C Gb B Eb Ab

I
C Gb Ab Eb

V
Eb Ab C Gb

X
Eb Ab C Gb

V
Eb Ab C Gb B

III
Ab C Gb C Eb

VI
Eb Ab Eb Gb C

XI
Eb Ab Eb Ab C Gb

VIII
Gb B Eb Ab C

IV
Ab Eb Gb C Eb Ab

VIII
Gb C Eb Ab

XI
Eb Ab Eb Gb C Eb

X
Ab C Gb B Eb

Ab m. 7

Ab-Cb-Eb-Gb

Ab 13 (-9)

Ab-C-Eb-Gb-Bbb-F

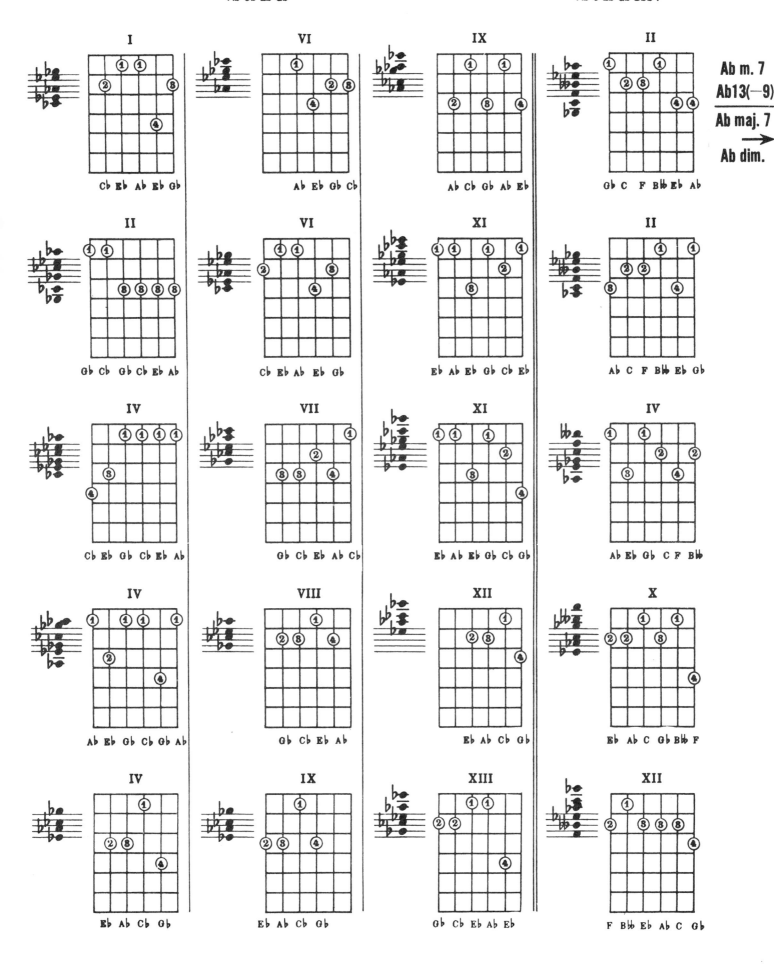

Ab m. 7
Ab13(—9)

Ab maj. 7

→

Ab dim.

Ab maj. 7

Ab-C-Eb-G

Ab dim.

Ab-Cb-Ebb-Gbb

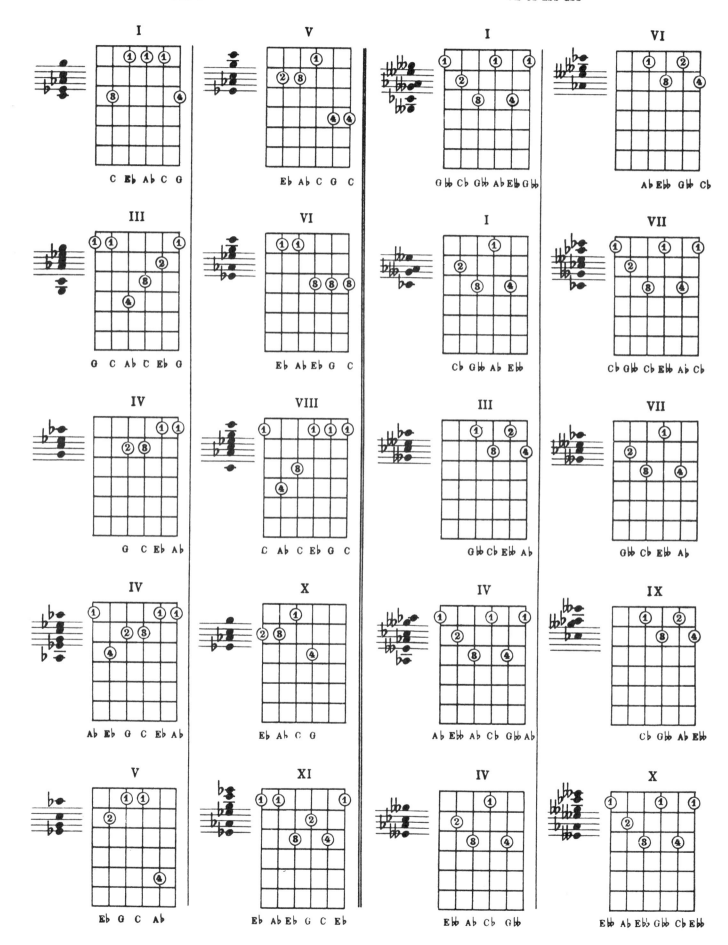

Ab 7 (+5)

Ab-C-E-Gb

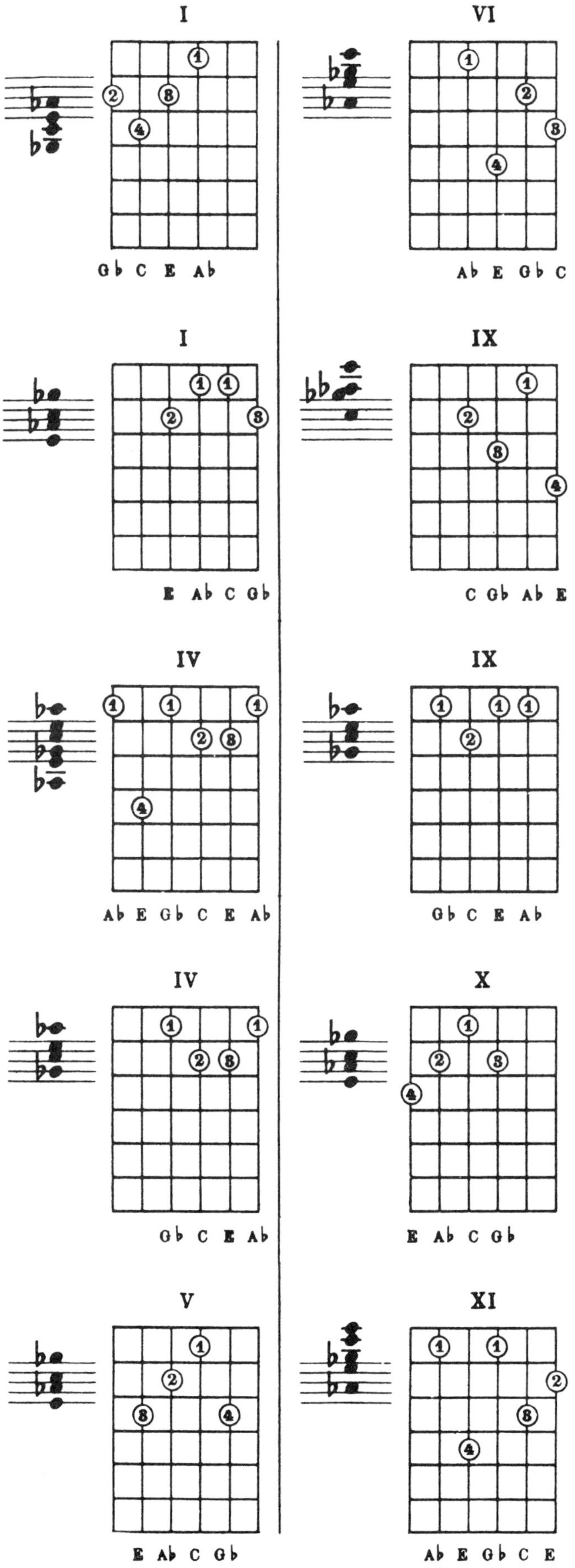

Ab 7 (-5)

Ab-C-Ebb-Gb

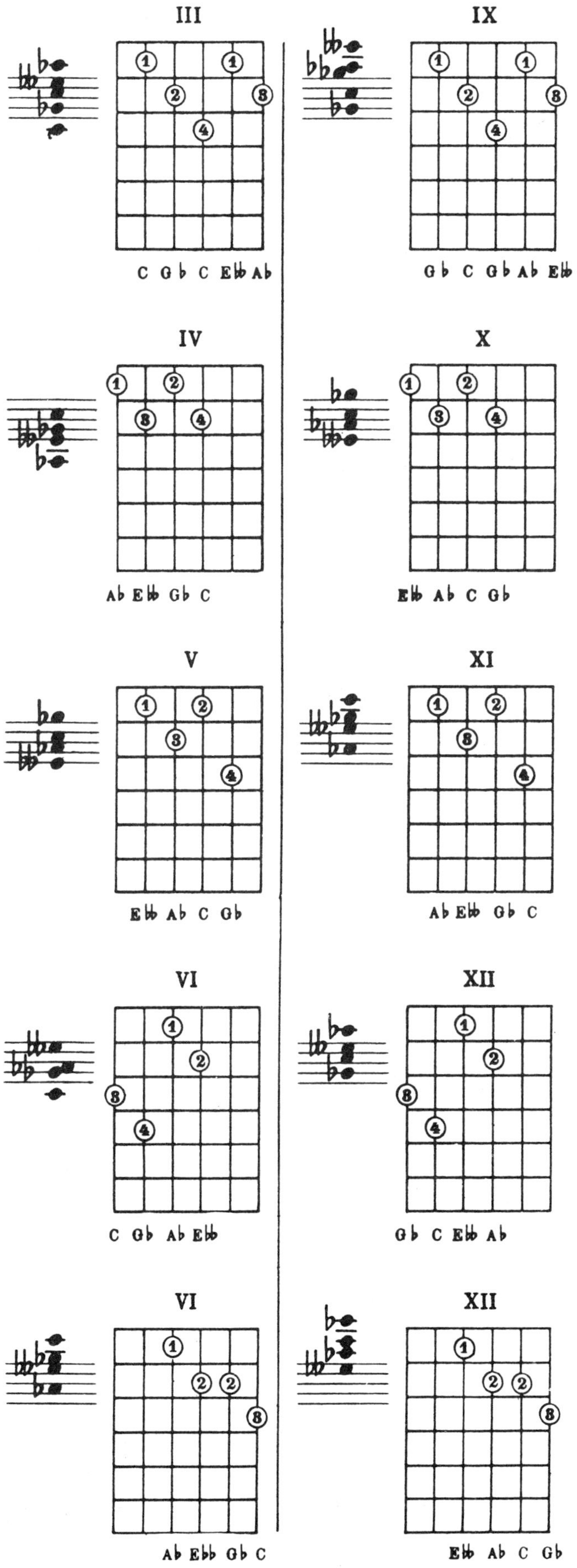

Ab 7 (+5)
Ab 7 (−5)

Ab 9

→

Ab 7 (−9)

Ab 9

Ab-C-Eb-Gb-Bb

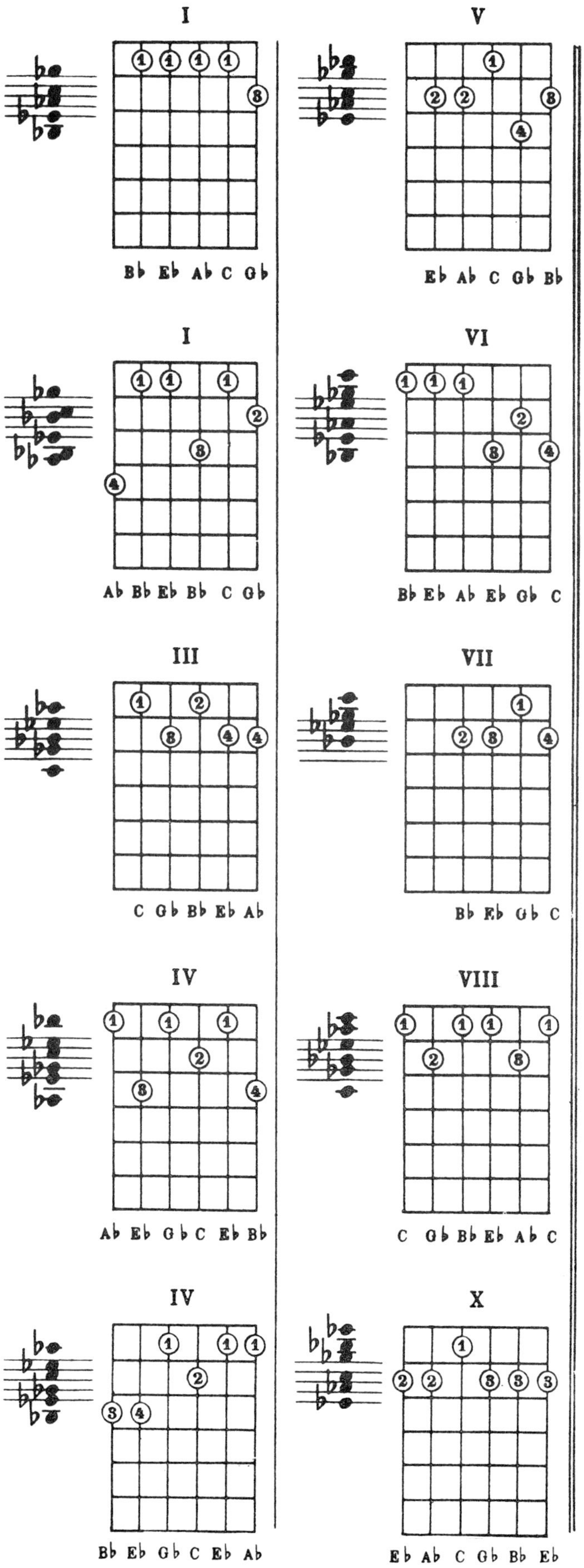

Ab 7 (-9)

Ab-C-Eb-Gb-Bbb

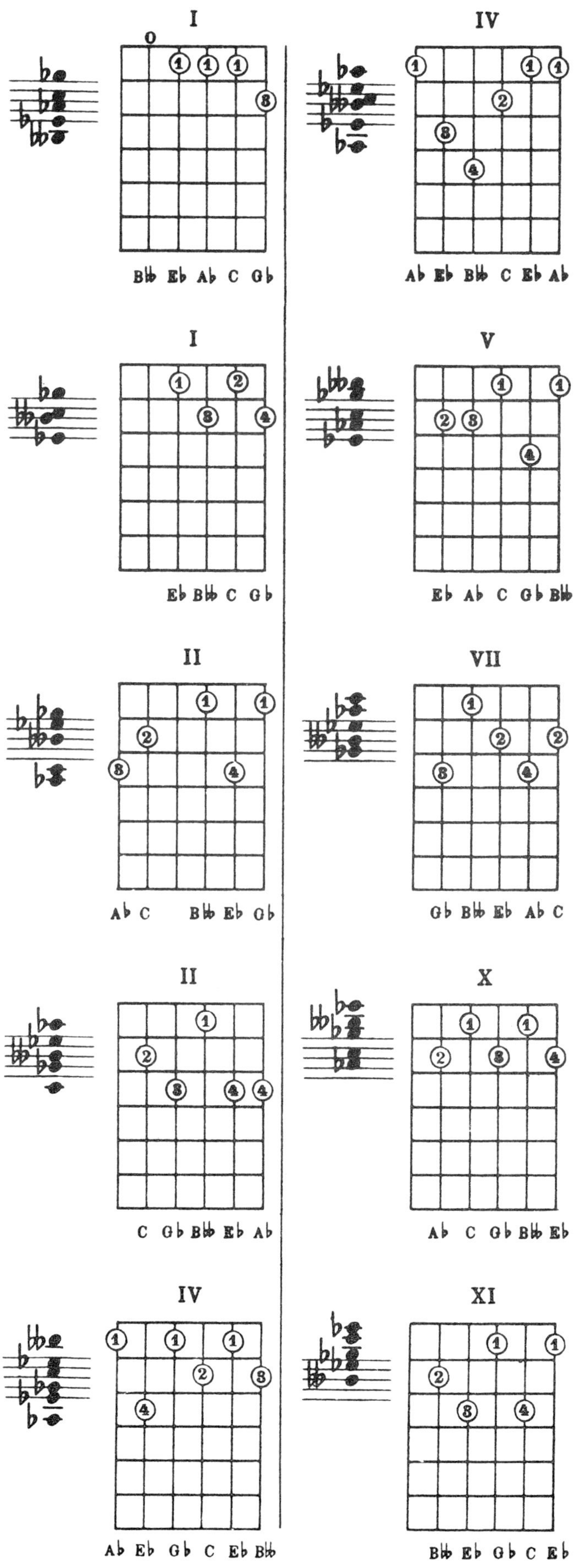

Ab 9 (+5)
Ab-C-E-Gb-Bb

Ab 9 (-5)
Ab-C-Ebb-Gb-Bb

Ab 9 (+5)
Ab 9 (−5)
Ab maj. 7 (add 9)
Ab 11
→
Ab aug. 11
Ab 13

Ab maj. 7 (add 9)
Ab-C-Eb-G-Bb

Ab 11
Ab-C-Eb-Gb-Bb-Db

Ab aug. 11
Ab-C-Eb-Gb-Bb-D

Ab 13
Ab-C-Eb-Gb-Bb-F

I
Bb Eb Ab C G

III
G C Ab Bb Eb G

VI
Eb Ab C G Bb

VI
Bb Eb Ab Eb G C

X
Ab C G Bb Eb

IV
Ab Db Gb C Eb Bb

VI
Bb Eb Ab Db Gb C

VIII
C Ab Db Gb Bb Eb

IX
Db Ab C Gb Bb Eb

XI
Eb Bb Db Ab C Gb

I
Bb Eb Ab D Gb

IV
Ab D Gb C Eb Bb

VI
Bb Eb Ab D Gb C

X
D Ab C Gb Bb Eb

X
Eb Ab C Gb Bb D

I
F Bb Eb Ab C Gb

II
Ab C F Bb Eb Gb

IV
Ab Eb Gb C F Bb

VI
Bb Eb Ab F Gb C

X
Eb Ab C Gb Bb F

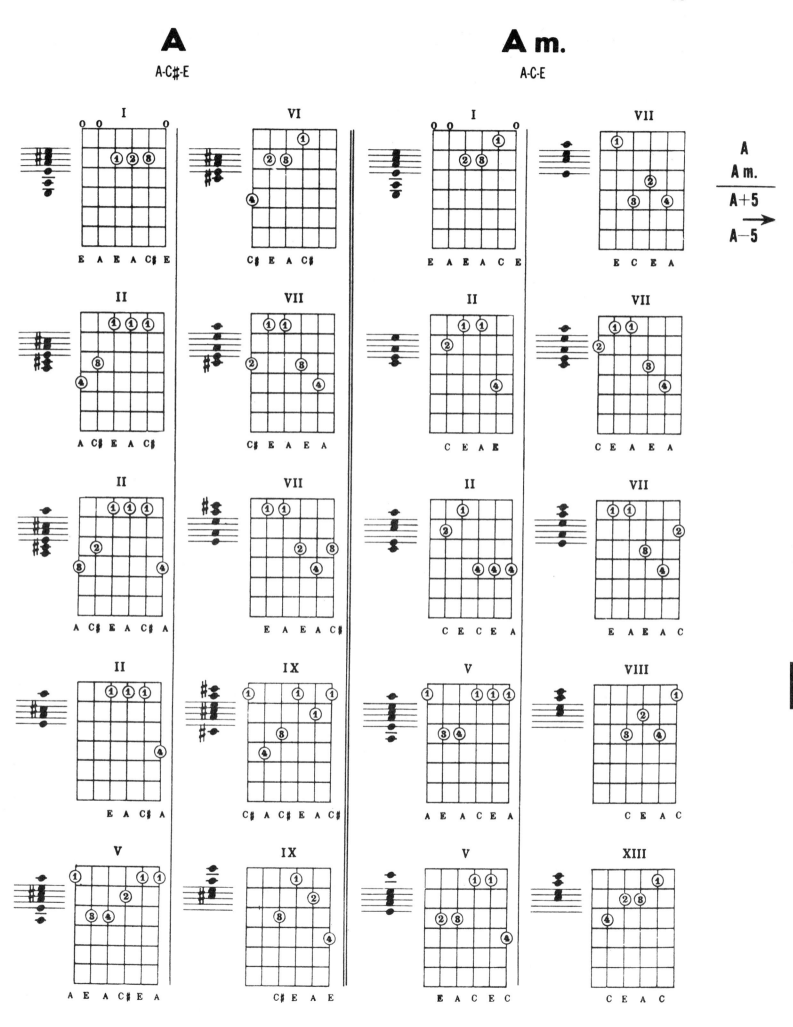

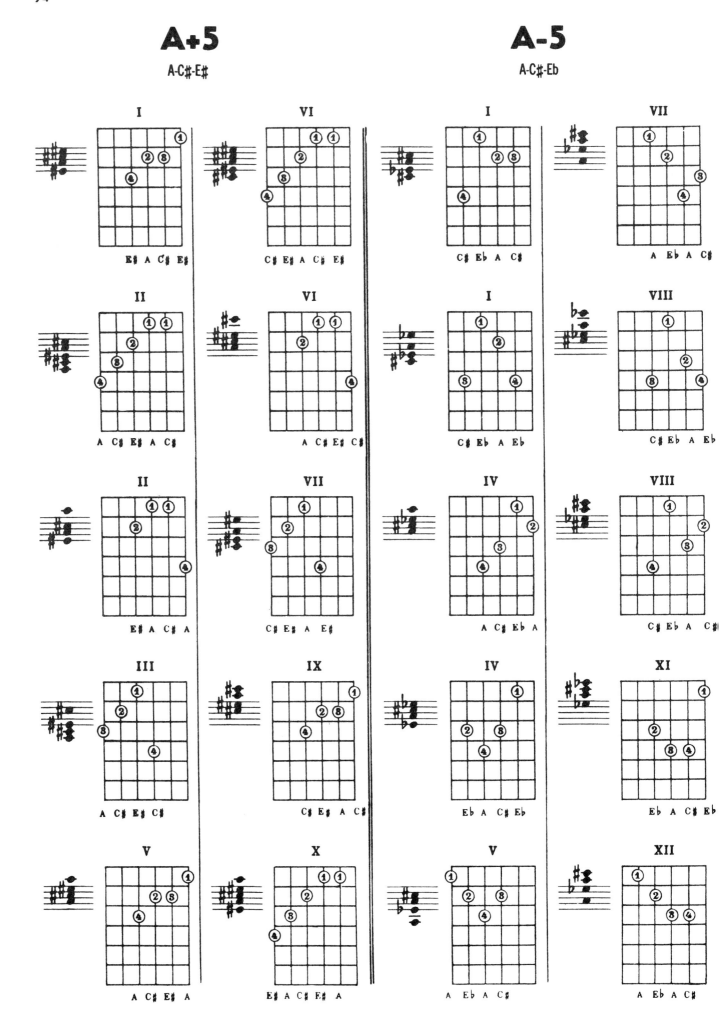

A 6
A-C#-E-F#

A m. 6
A-C-E-F#

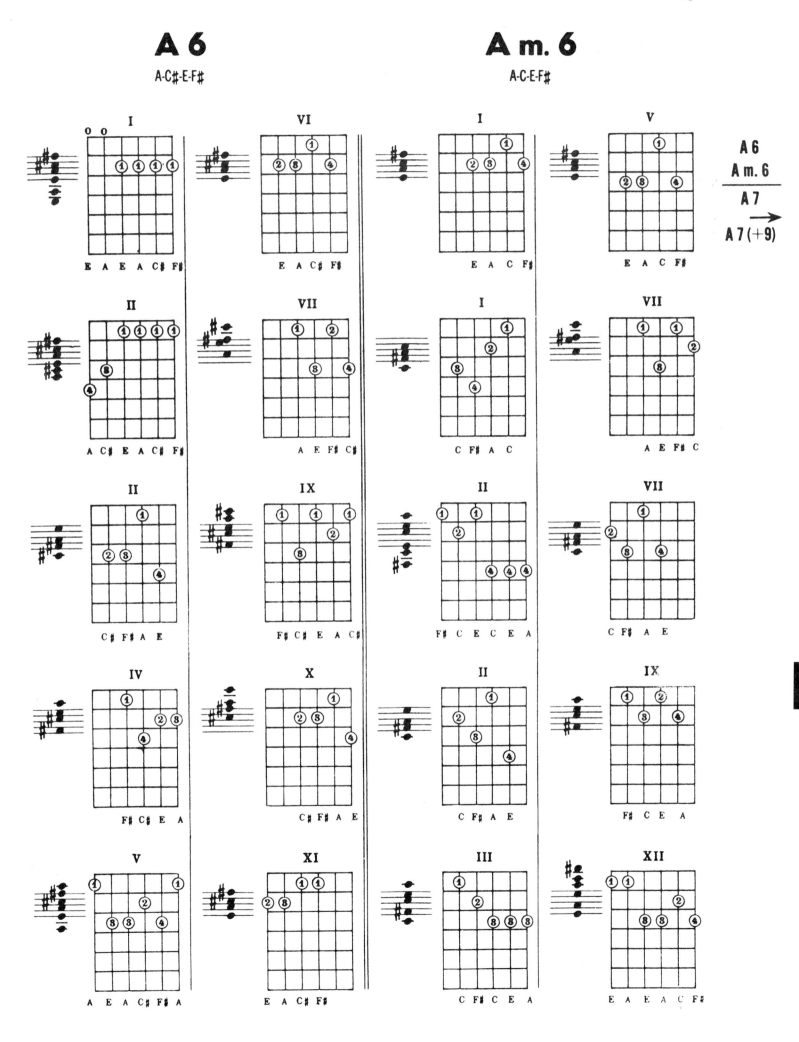

A 6
A m. 6
―――
A 7
⟶
A 7 (+9)

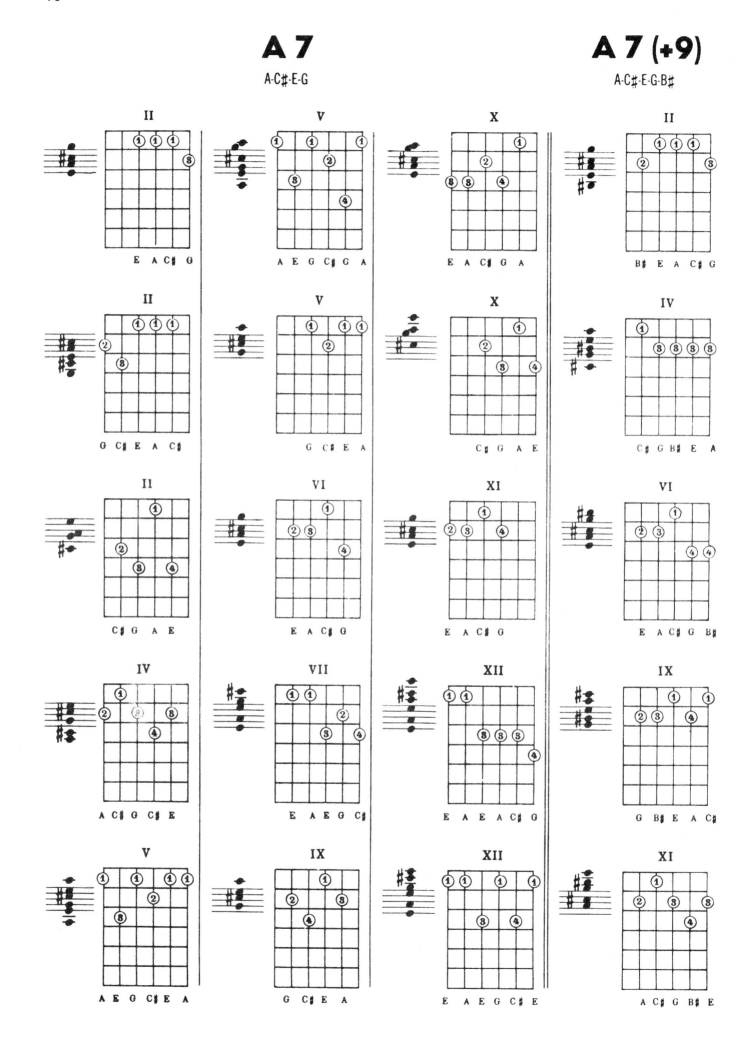

A m. 7
A-C-E-G

A 13 (-9)
A-C#-E-G-Bb-F#

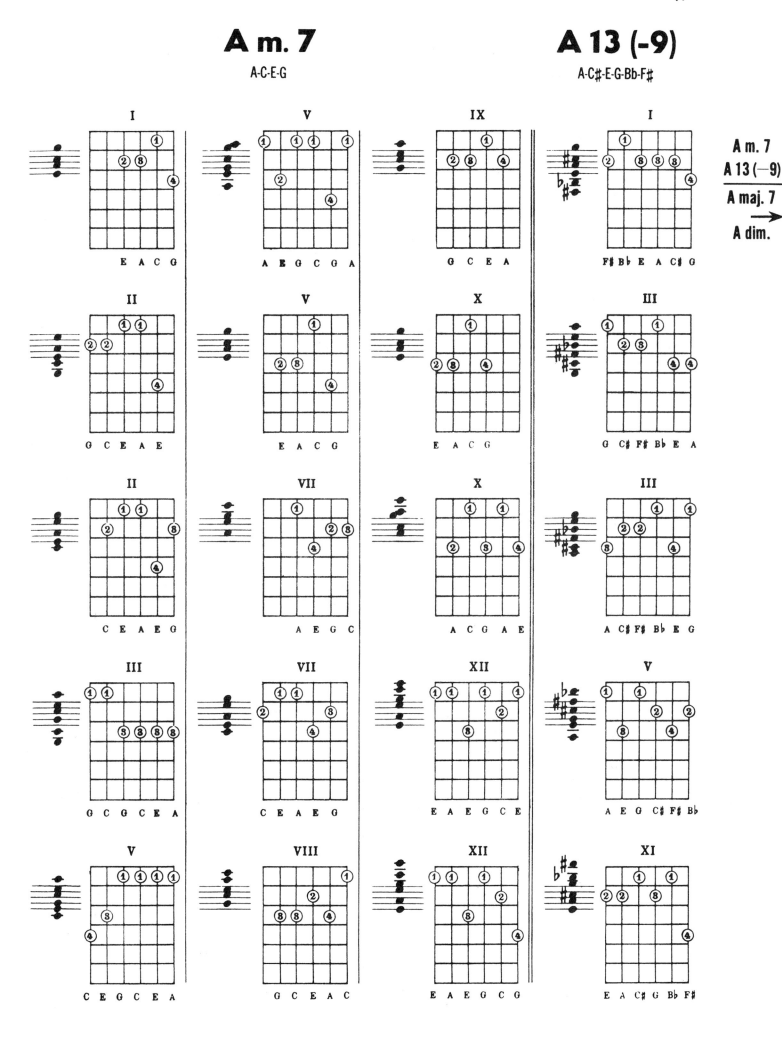

A m. 7
A 13 (—9)
A maj. 7
→
A dim.

A maj. 7

A-C♯-E-G♯

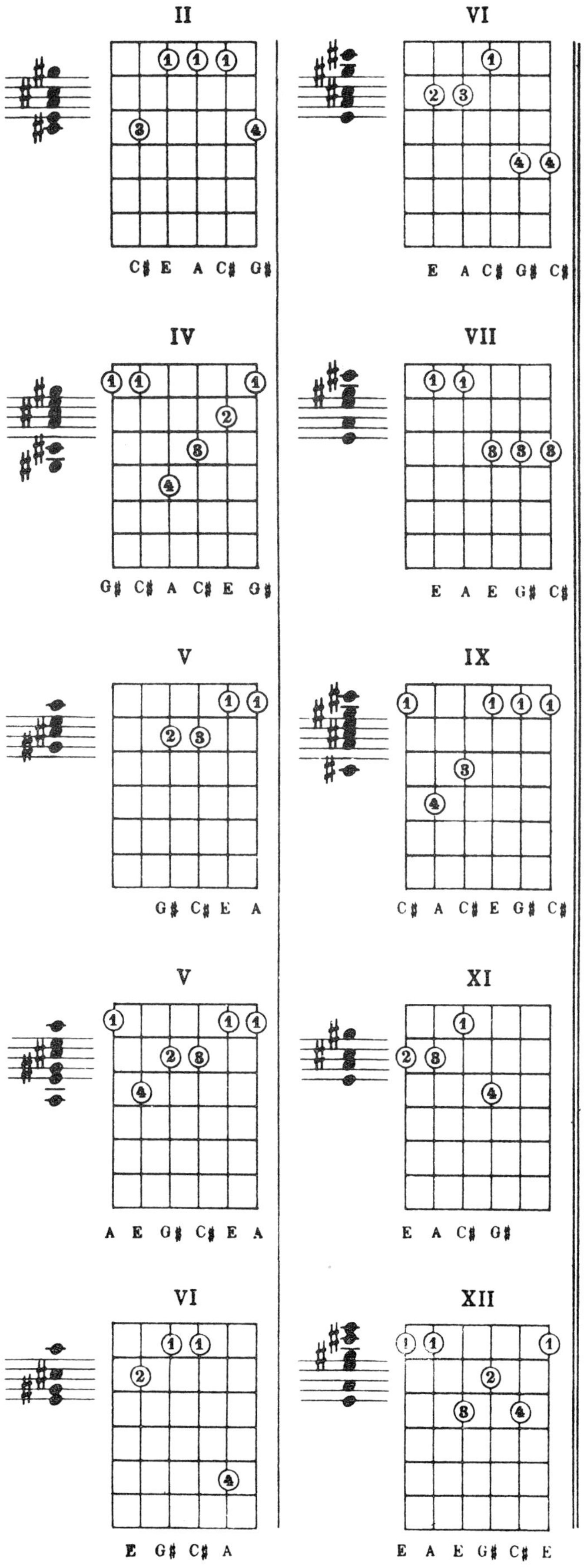

A dim.

A-C-Eb-Gb

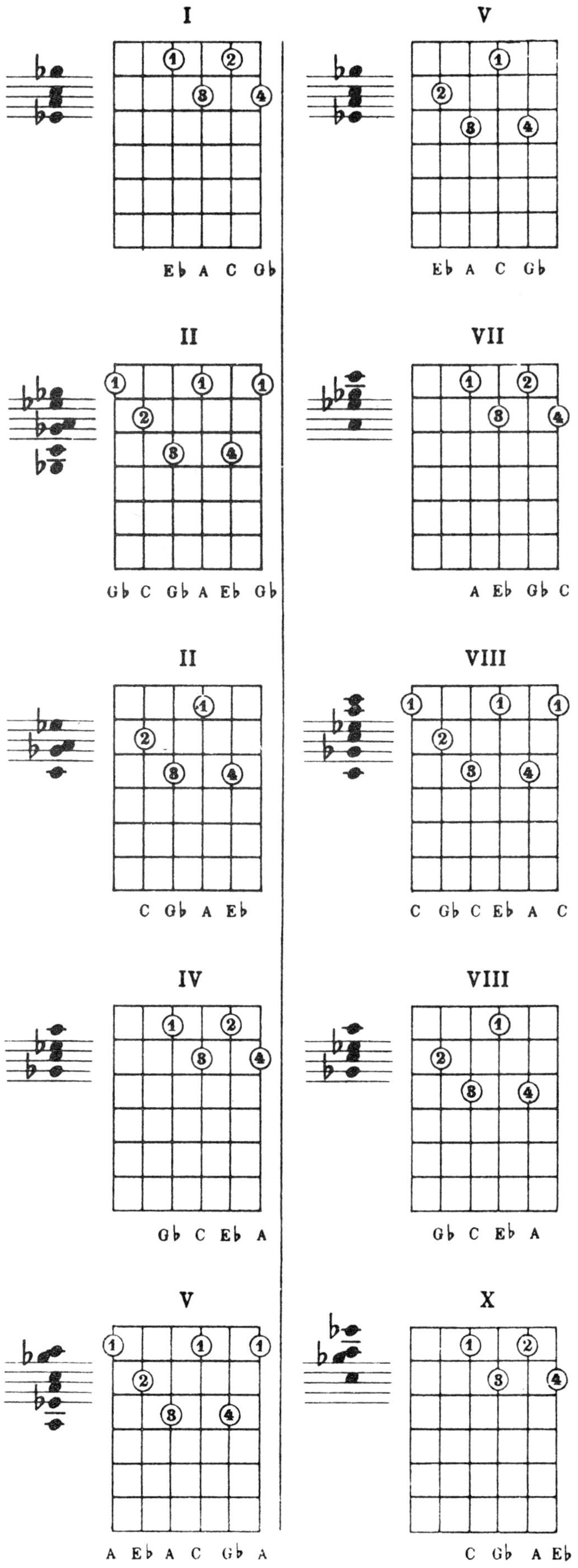

A 7 (+5)
A-C#-E#-G

A 7 (-5)
A-C#-Eb-G

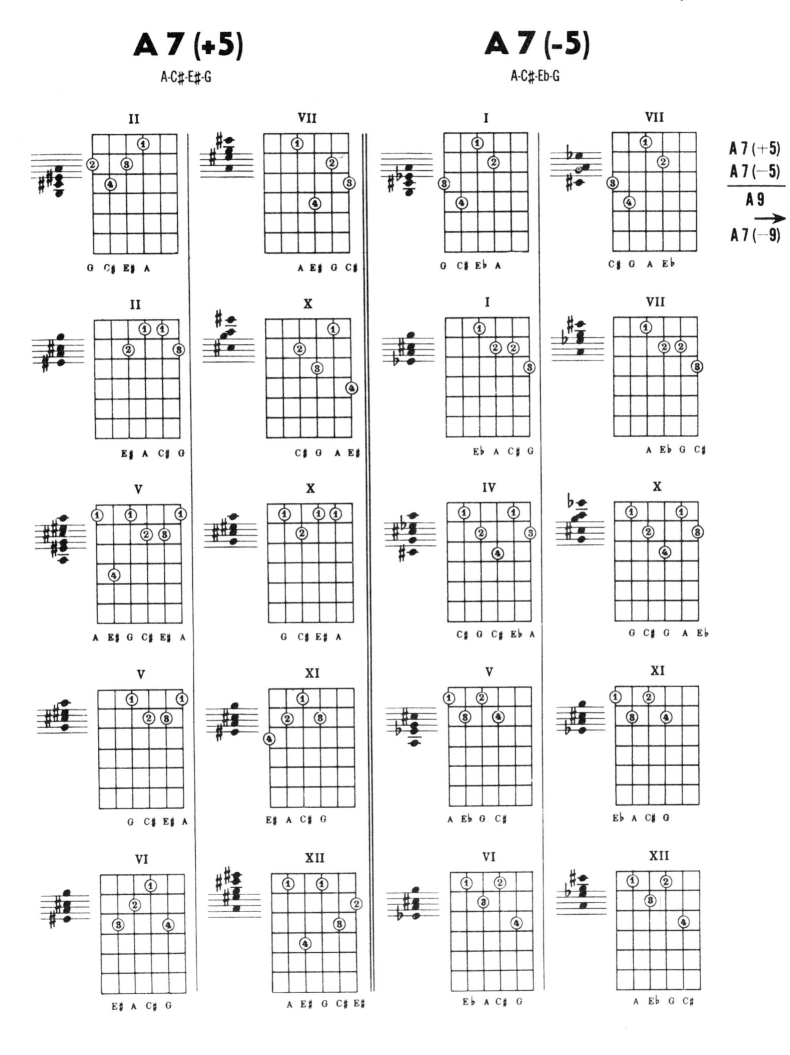

A9
A-C#-E-G-B

A7 (-9)
A-C#-E-G-Bb

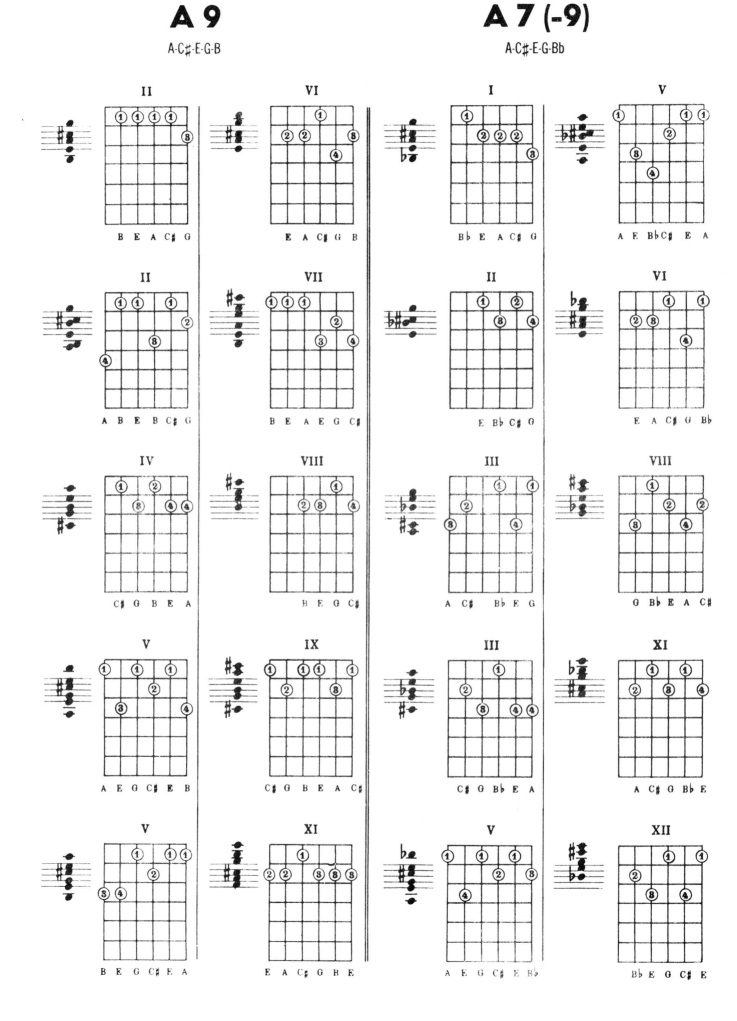

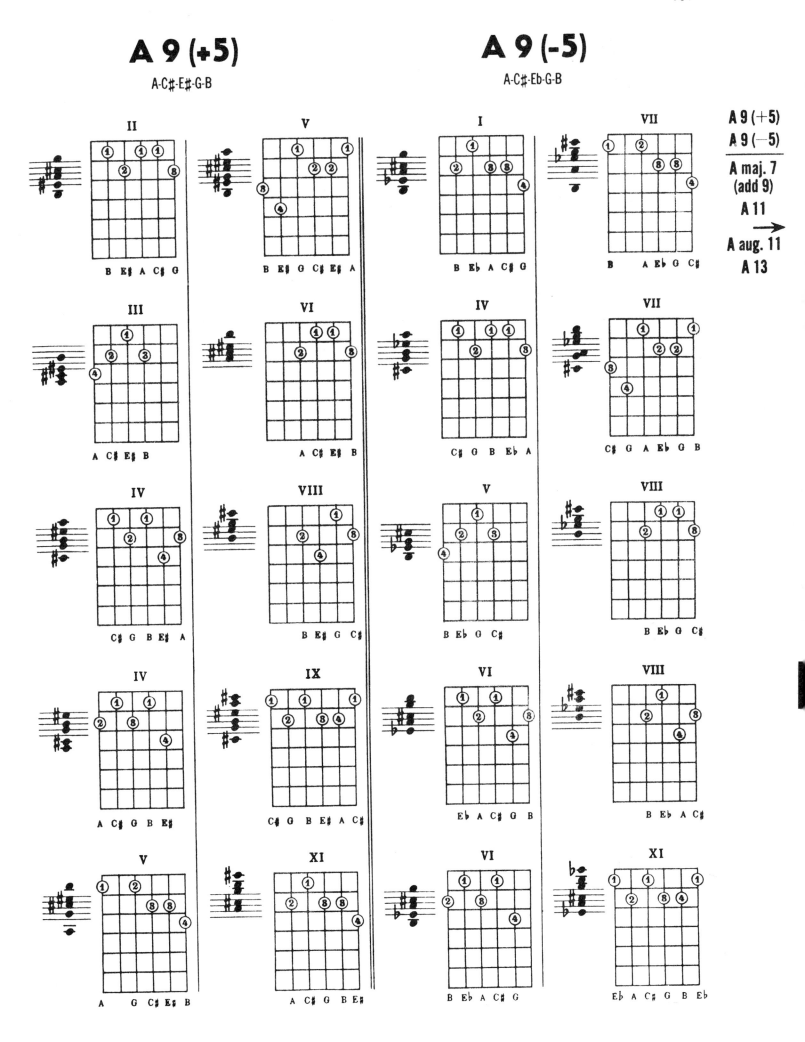

A maj. 7 (add 9)
A-C♯-E-G♯-B

A 11
A-C♯-E-G-B-D

A aug. 11
A-C♯-E-G-B-D♯

A 13
A-C♯-E-G-B-F♯

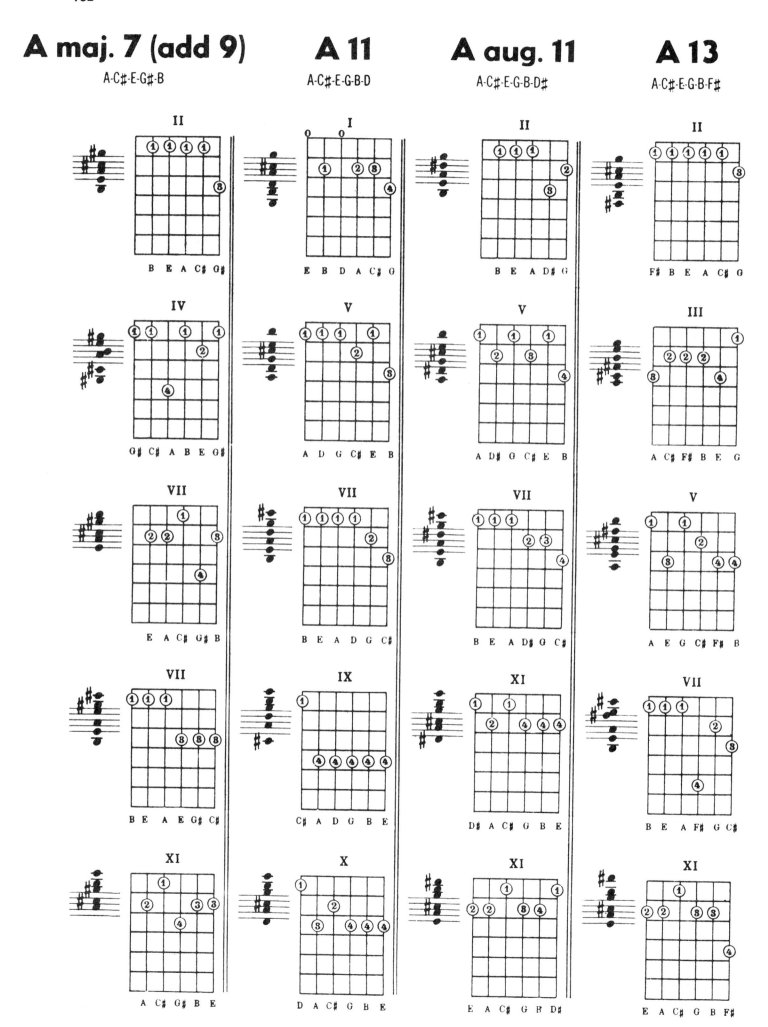

Bb

Bb-D-F

Bb m.

Bb-Db-F

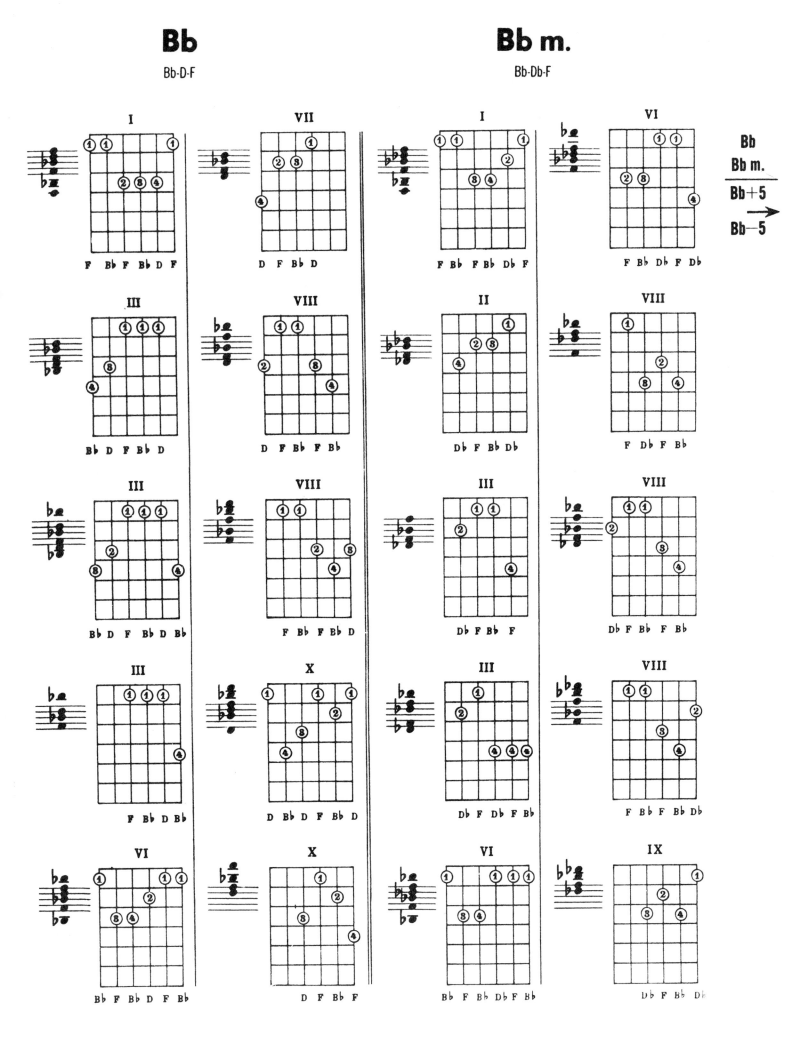

Bb
Bb m.
Bb+5 →
Bb—5

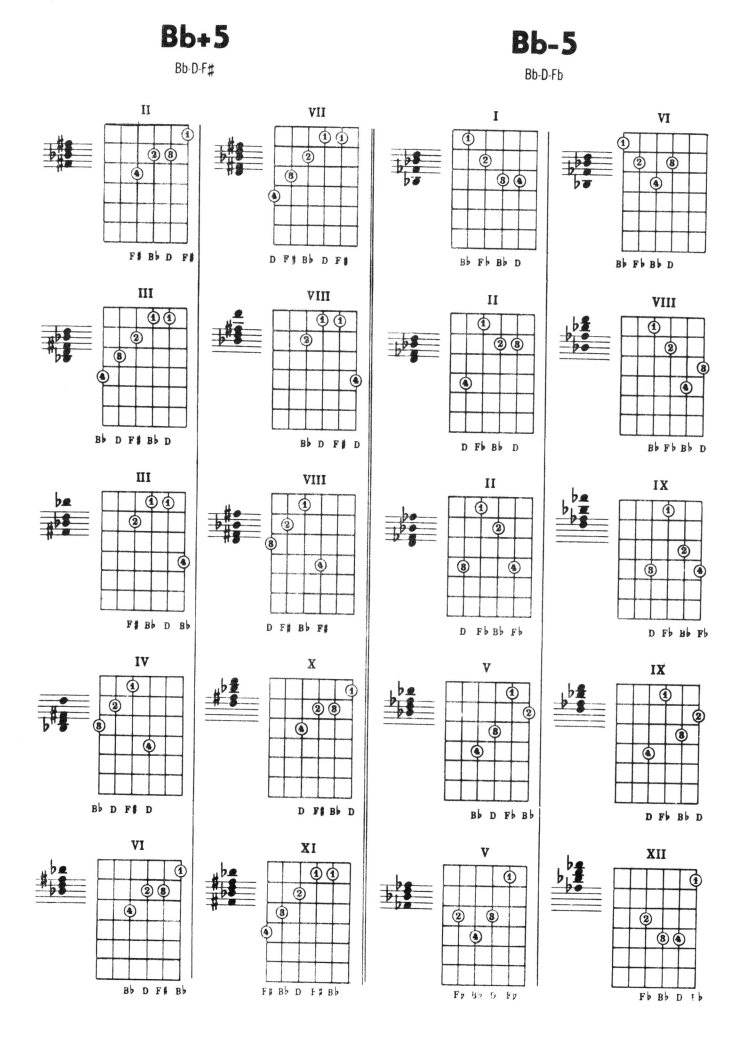

Bb 6

Bb-D-F-G

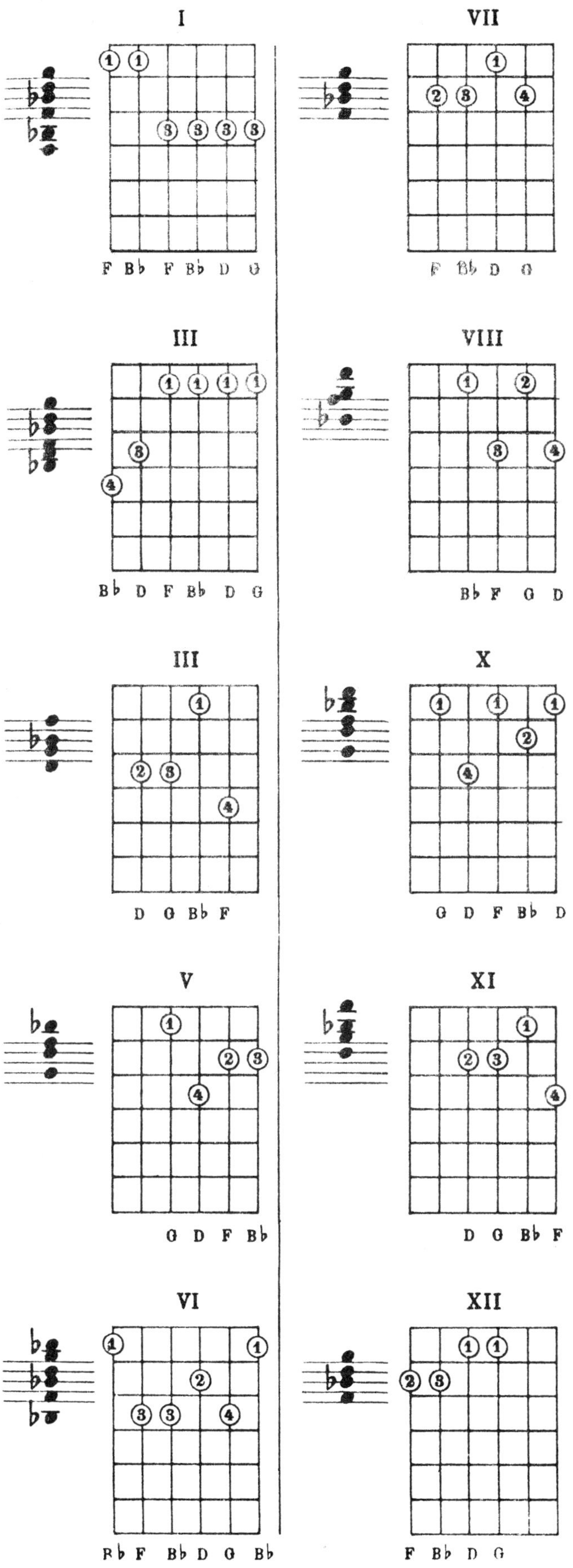

Bb m. 6

Bb-Db-F-G

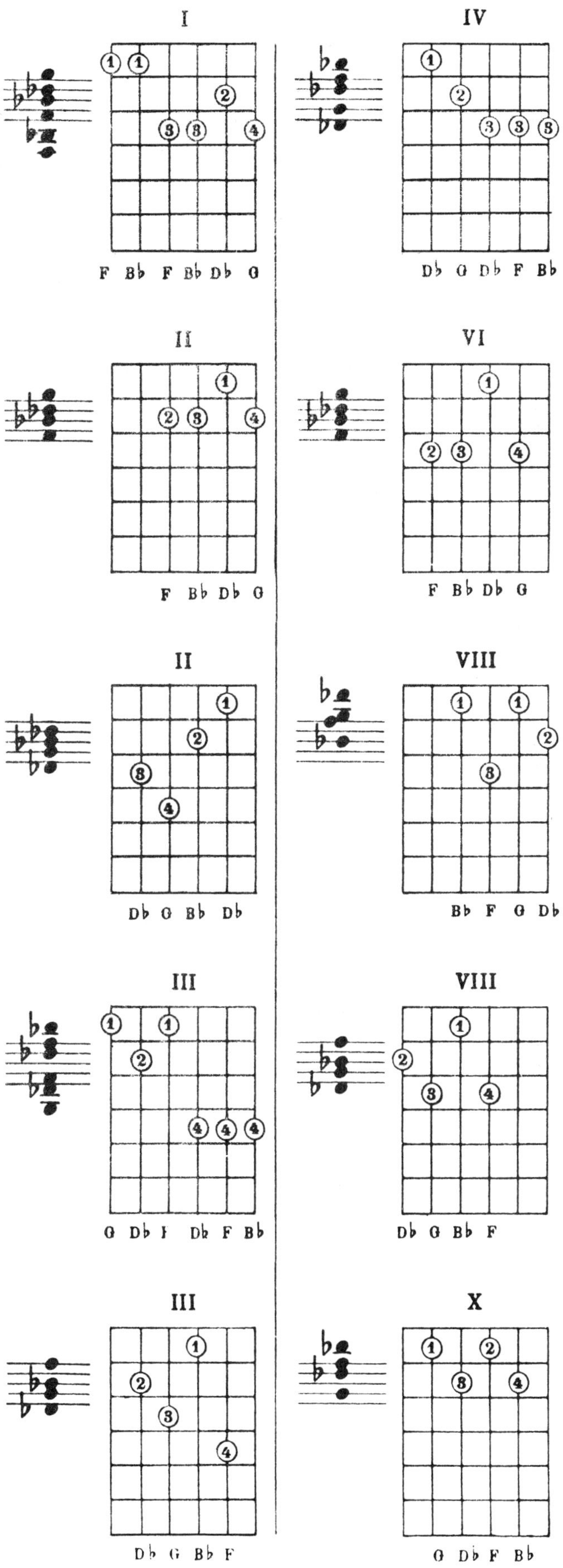

Bb 6
Bb m. 6

Bb 7
→
Bb 7 (+9)

Bb 7

Bb-D-F-Ab

Bb 7 (+9)

Bb-D-F-Ab-C♯

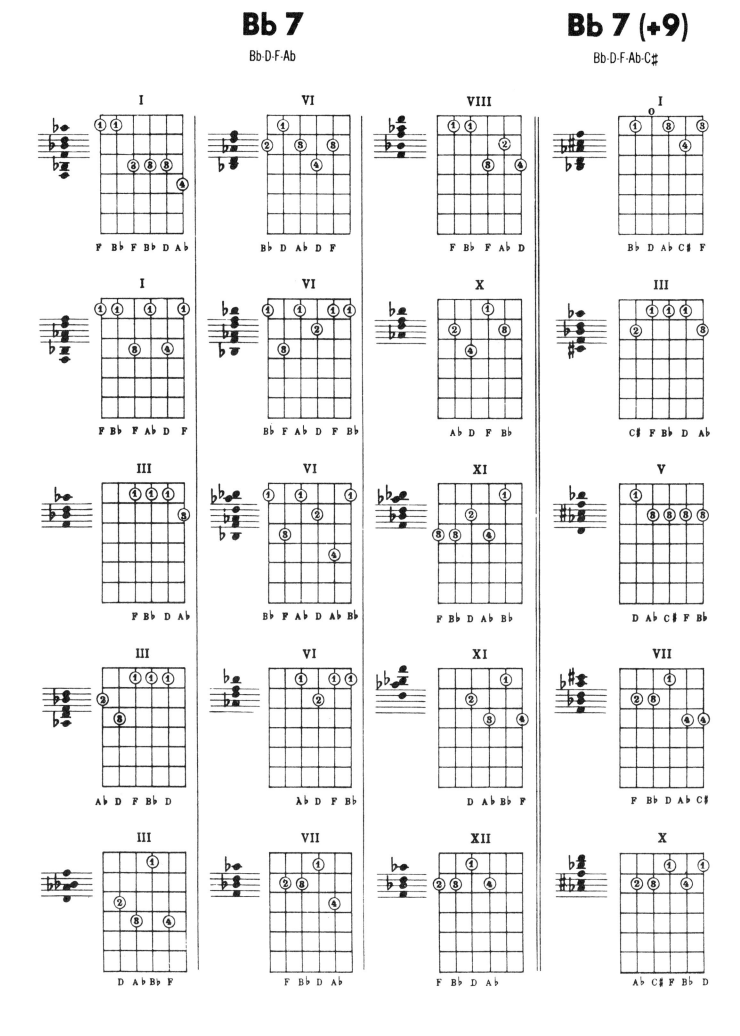

Bb m. 7

Bb-Db-F-Ab

Bb 13 (-9)

Bb-D-F-Ab-Cb-G

Bb m. 7
Bb 13(−9)
—
Bb maj. 7
→
Bb dim.

Column 1 (Bb m. 7):

I — F Bb F Ab Db F

I — F Bb F Ab Db Ab

II — F Bb Db Ab

III — Ab Db F Bb F

III — Db F Bb F Ab

Column 2 (Bb m. 7):

IV — Ab Db Ab Db F Bb

VI — Db F Ab Db F Bb

VI — Bb F Ab Db Ab Bb

VI — F Bb Db Ab

VIII — Bb F Ab Db

Column 3 (Bb m. 7):

VIII — Db F Bb F Ab

IX — Ab Db F Bb Db

X — Ab Db F Bb

XI — F Bb Db Ab

XI — Bb Db Ab Bb F

Column 4 (Bb 13 (−9)):

II — G Cb F Bb D Ab

IV — Ab D G Cb F Bb

IV — Bb D G Cb F Ab

VI — Bb F Ab D G Cb

XII — F Bb D Ab Cb G

Bb maj. 7

Bb-D-F-A

Bb dim.

Bb-Db-Fb-Abb

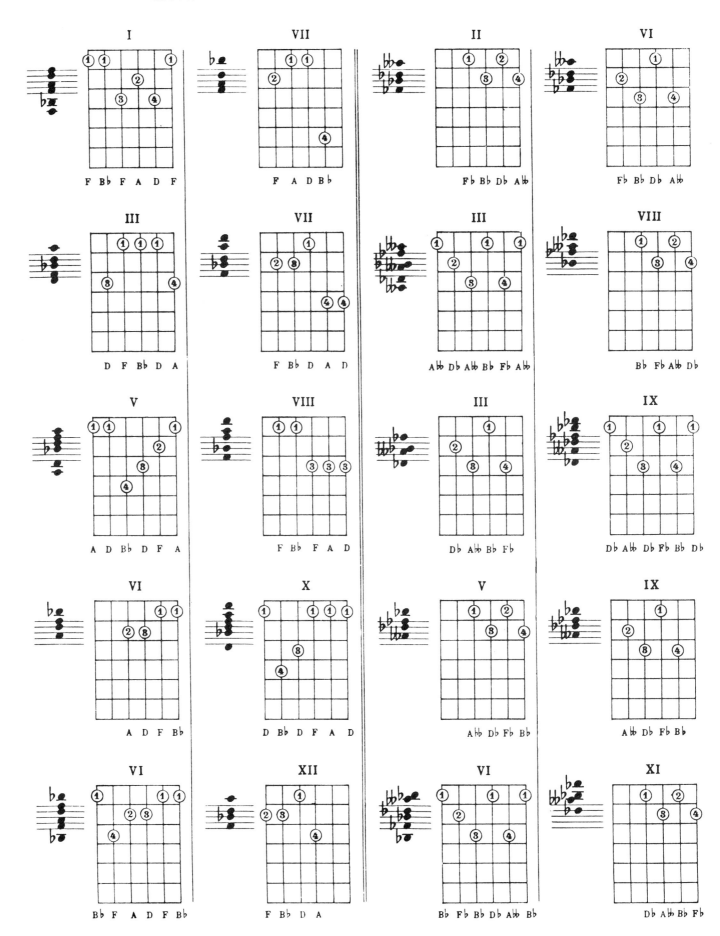

Bb 7 (+5)

Bb-D-F♯-Ab

Bb 7 (-5)

Bb-D-Fb-Ab

I

Bb F♯ Ab D F♯

VII

F♯ Bb D Ab

III

Ab D F♯ Bb

VIII

Bb F♯ Ab D

III

F♯ Bb D Ab

XI

D Ab Bb F♯

VI

Bb F♯ Ab D F♯ Bb

XI

Ab D F♯ Bb

VI

Ab D F♯ Bb

XII

F♯ Bb D Ab

I

Bb Fb Ab D

VII

Fb Bb D Ab

II

Ab D Fb Bb

VIII

D Ab Bb Fb

II

Fb Bb D Ab

VIII

Bb Fb Ab D

V

D Ab D Fb Bb

XI

Ab D Ab Bb Fb

VI

Bb Fb Ab D

XII

Fb Bb D Ab

Bb 7 (+5)
Bb 7 (−5)
_____
Bb 9
→
Bb 7 (−9)

Bb 9

Bb-D-F-Ab-C

Bb 7 (-9)

Bb-D-F-Ab-Cb

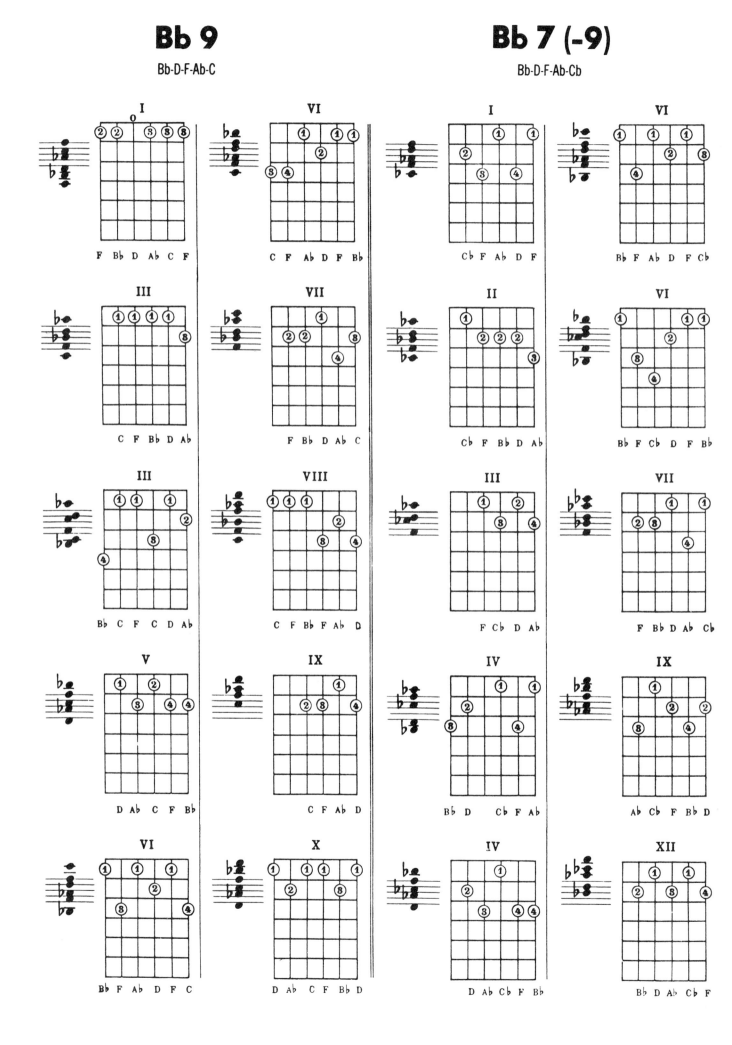

Bb 9 (+5)
Bb-D-F#-Ab-C

Bb 9 (-5)
Bb-D-Fb-Ab-C

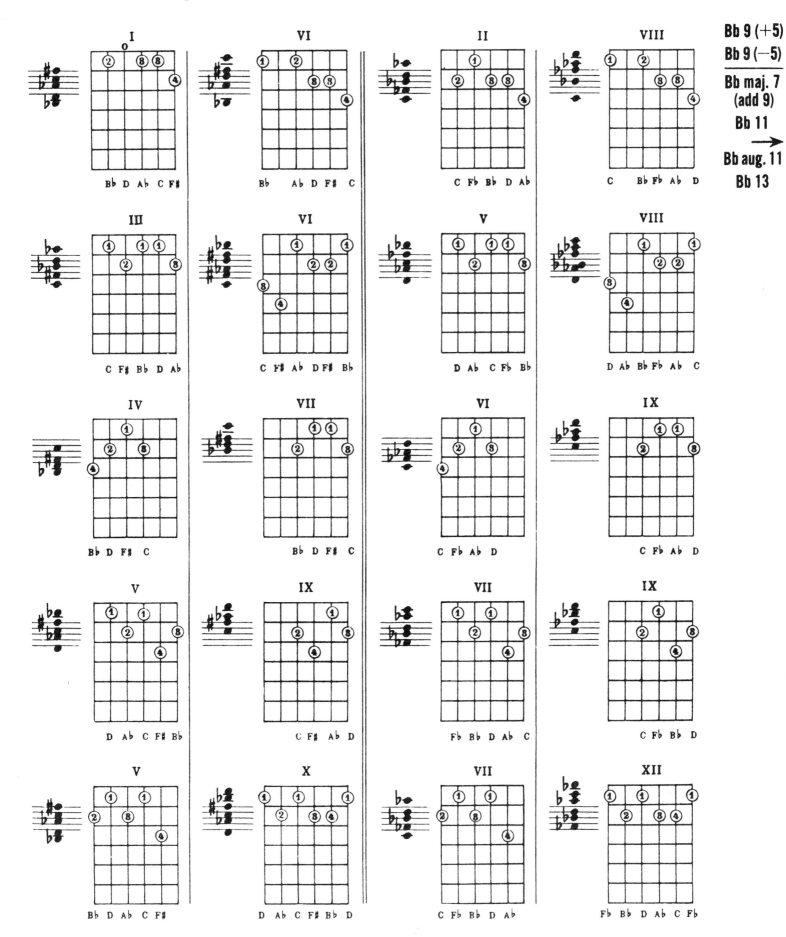

Bb 9 (+5)
Bb 9 (—5)

Bb maj. 7 (add 9)

Bb 11
→
Bb aug. 11
Bb 13

Bb maj. 7 (add 9)
Bb-D-F-A-C

Bb 11
Bb-D-F-Ab-C-Eb

Bb aug. 11
Bb-D-F-Ab-C-E

Bb 13
Bb-D-F-Ab-C-G

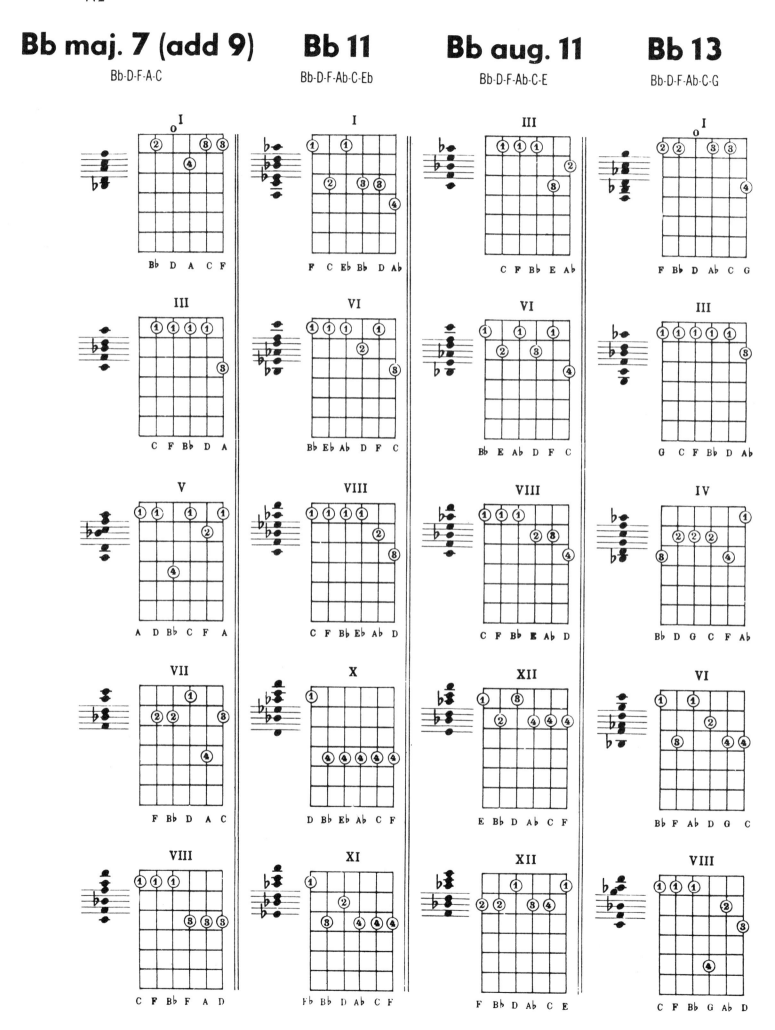

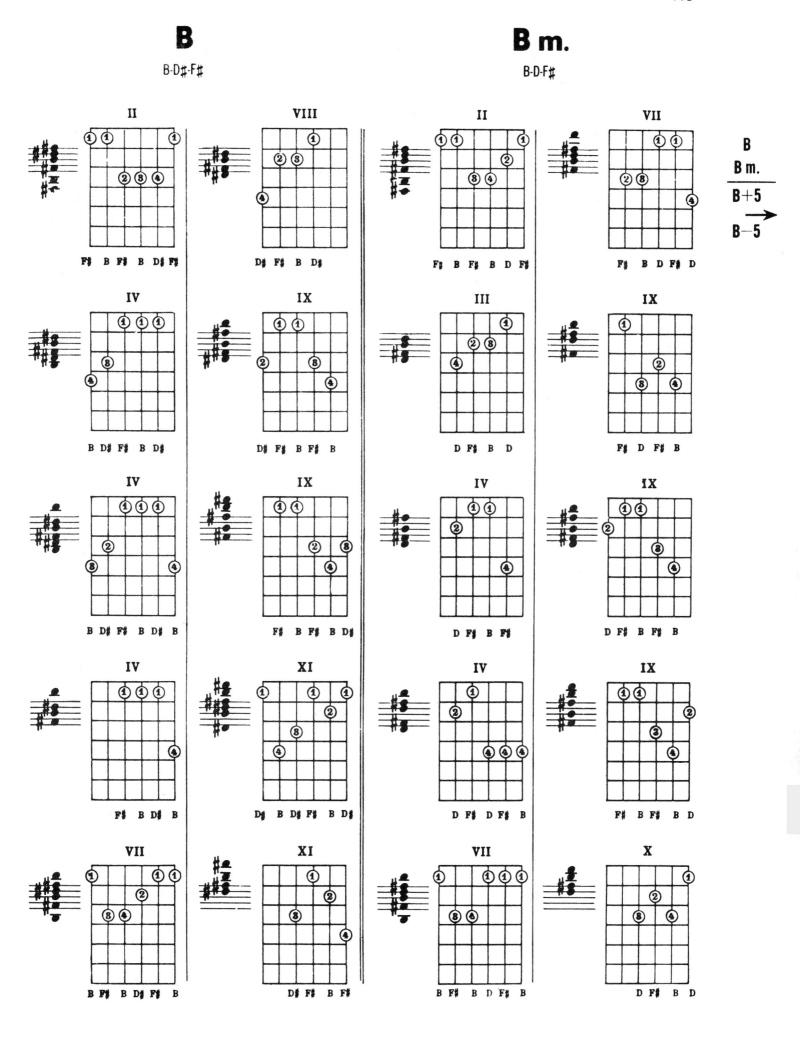

B+5

B-D♯-F×

B-5

B-D♯-F

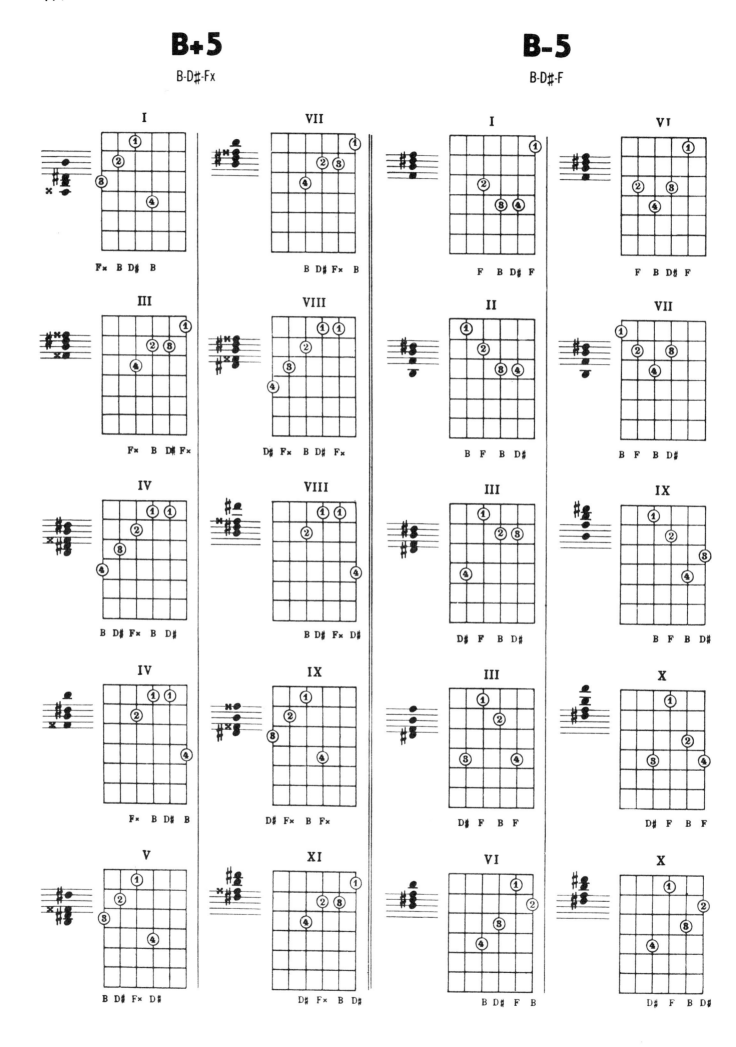

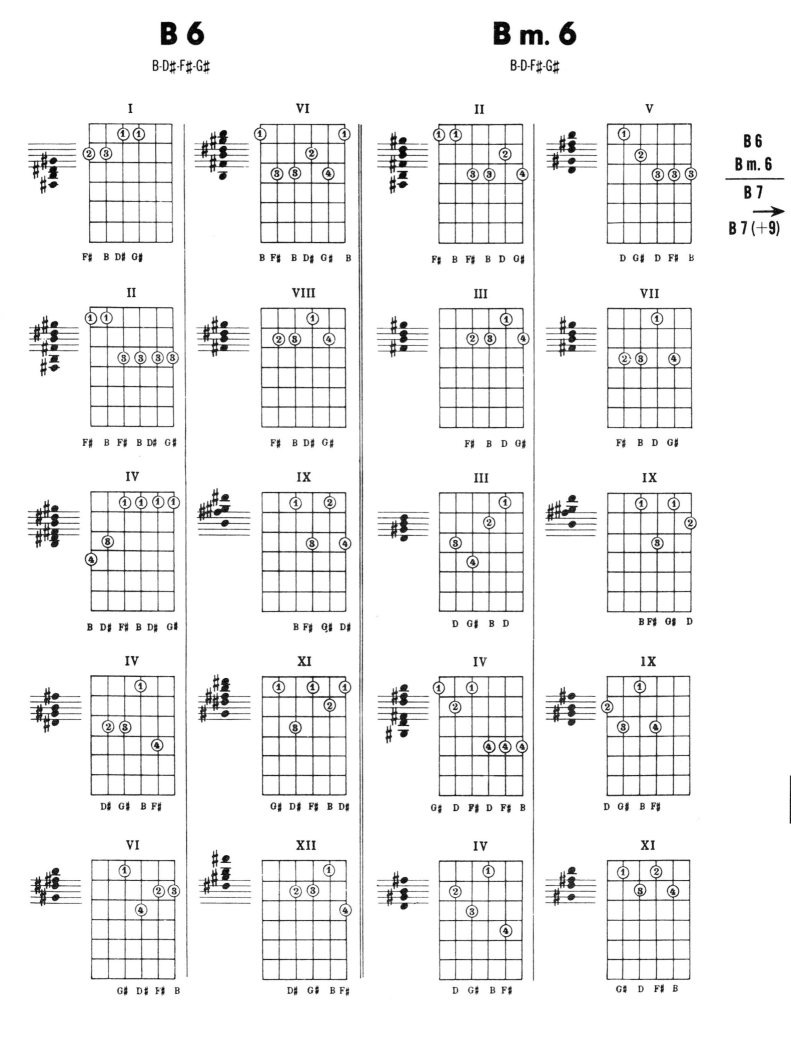

B 7

B-D#-F#-A

B 7 (+9)

B-D#-F#-A-C×

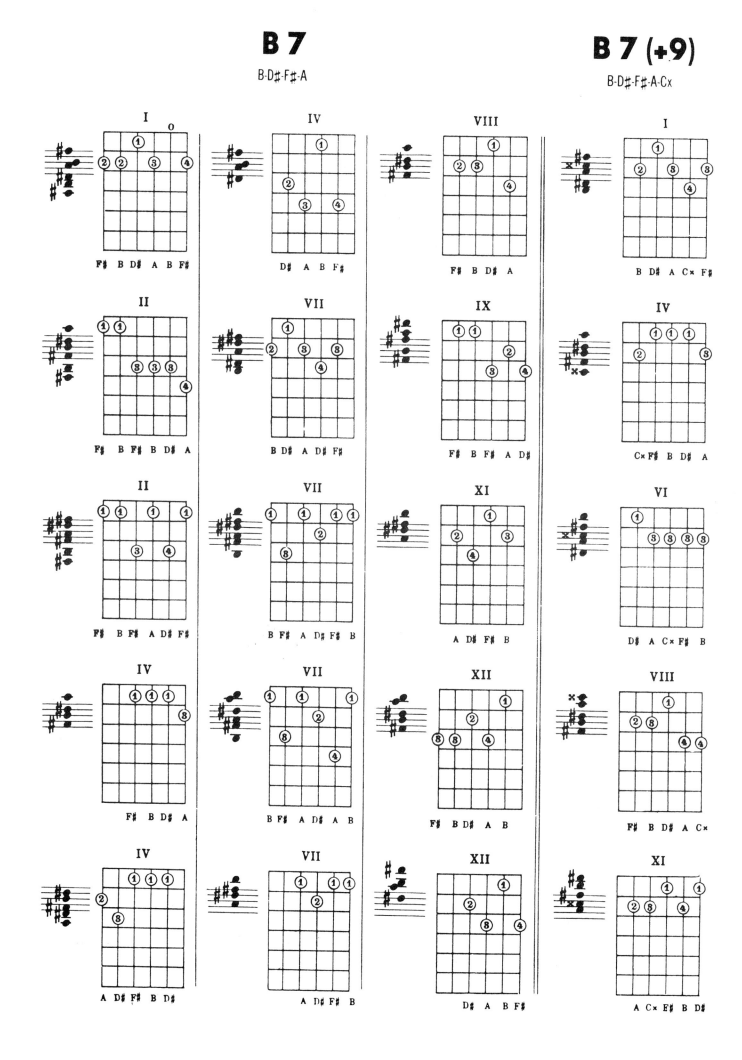

B m. 7

B-D-F#-A

B 13 (-9)

B-D#-F#-A-C-G#

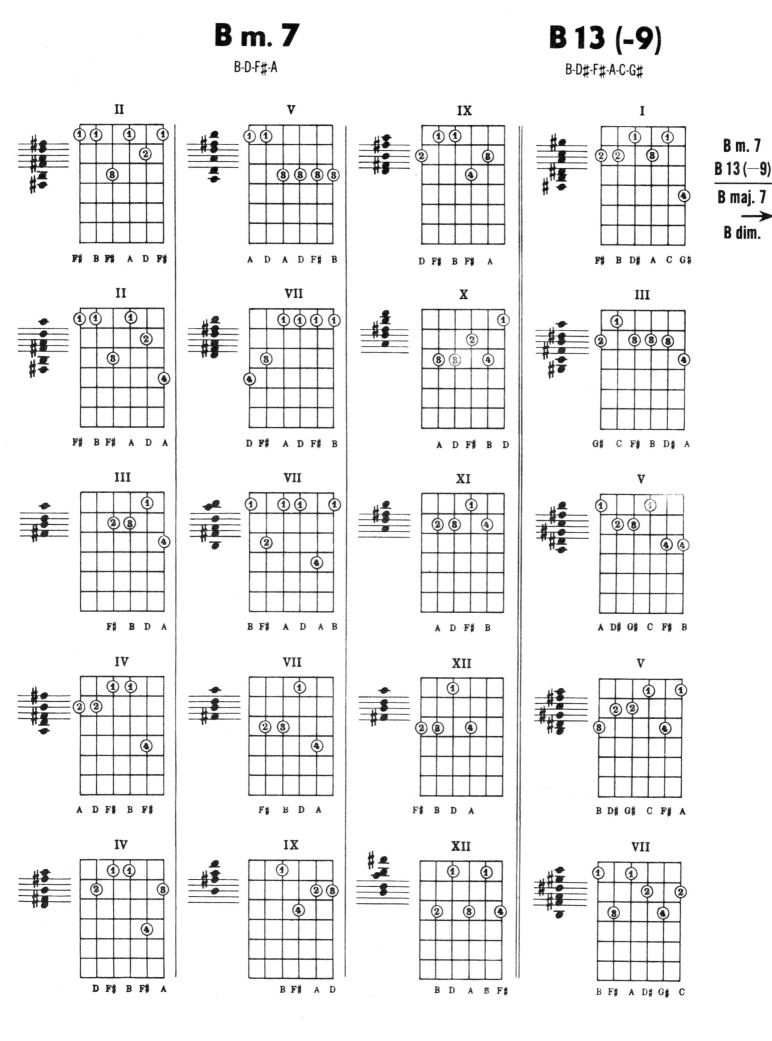

B m. 7
B 13 (−9)
───────
B maj. 7
→
B dim.

B maj. 7
B-D#-F#-A#

B dim.
B-D-F-Ab

B maj. 7

I

F# B D# A#

VII

B F# A# D# F# B

II

F# B F# A# D# F#

VIII

F# A# D# B

IV

D# F# B D# A#

VIII

F# B D# A# D#

VI

A# D# B D# F# A#

IX

F# B F# A# D#

VII

A# D# F# B

XI

D# B D# F# A# D#

B dim.

I

F B F Ab D F

VI

Ab D F B

I

B F Ab D

VII

B F B D Ab B

III

F B D Ab

VII

F B D Ab

IV

Ab D Ab B F Ab

IX

B F Ab D

IV

D Ab B F

X

D Ab D F B D

B 7 (+5)
B-D♯-F×-A

B 7 (-5)
B-D♯-F-A

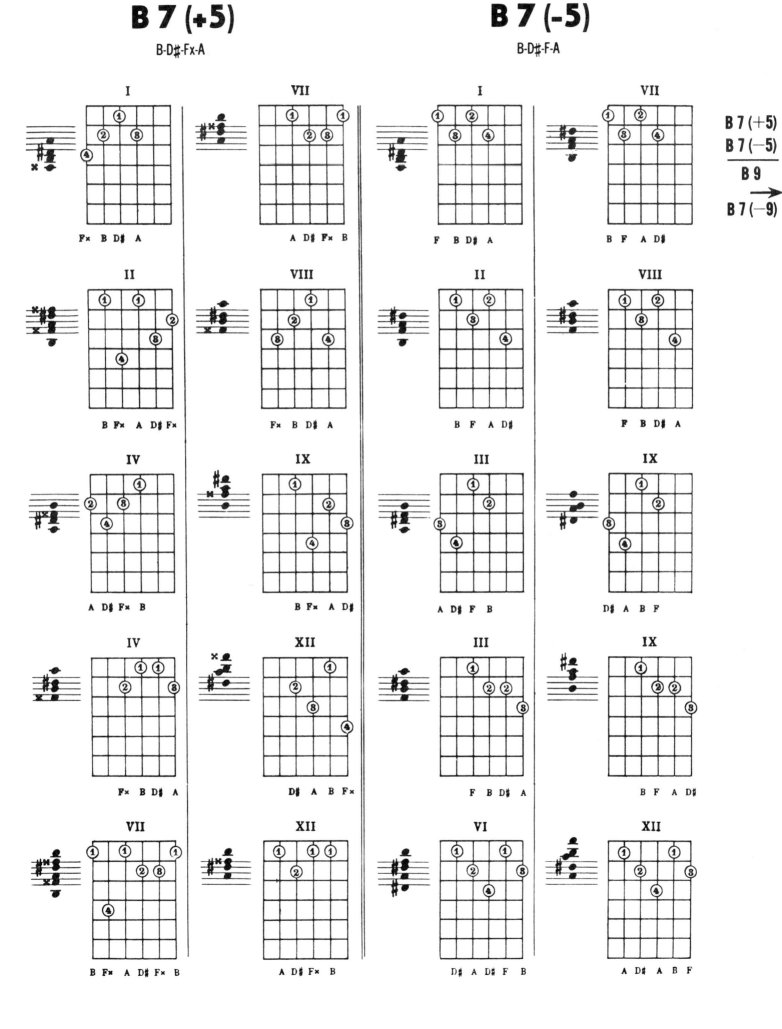

B 7 (+5)
B 7 (-5)
─────
B 9
→
B 7 (-9)

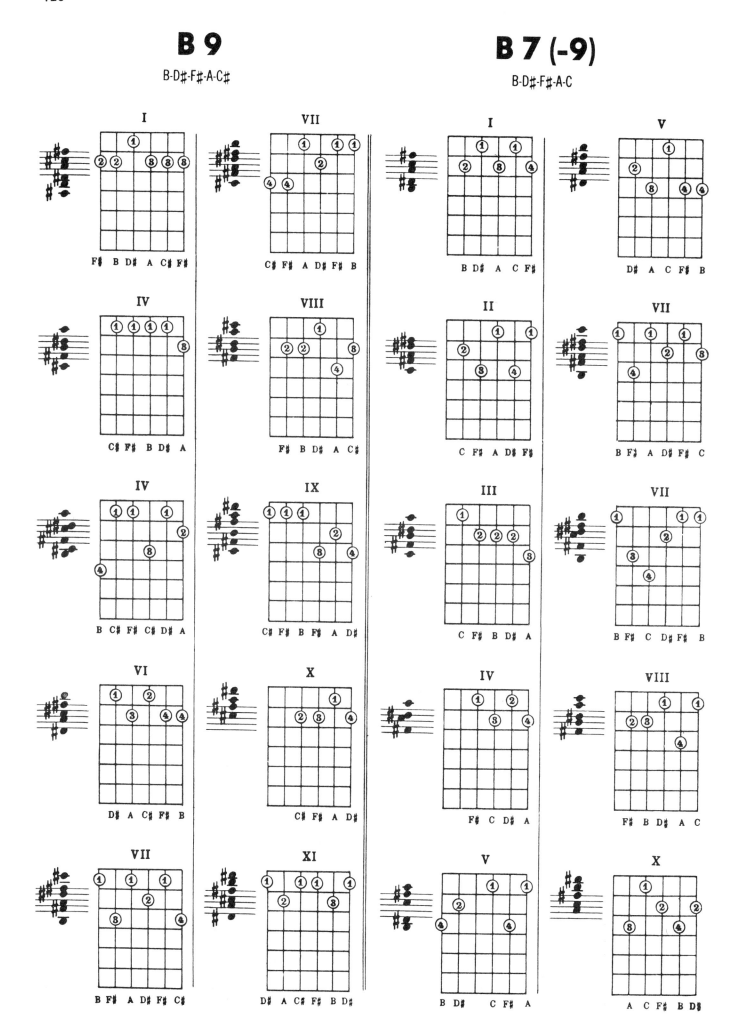

B 9 (+5)

B-D♯-F×-A-C♯

B 9 (-5)

B-D♯-F-A-C♯

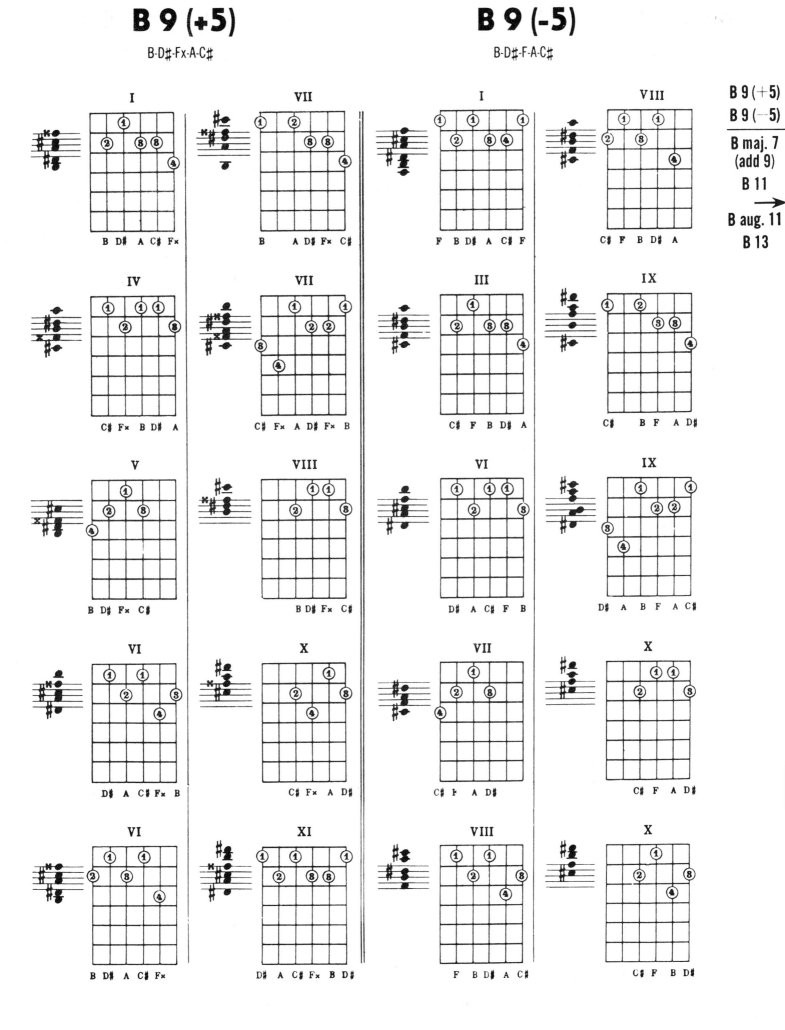

B 9 (+5)
B 9 (--5)
B maj. 7 (add 9)
B 11
→
B aug. 11
B 13

122

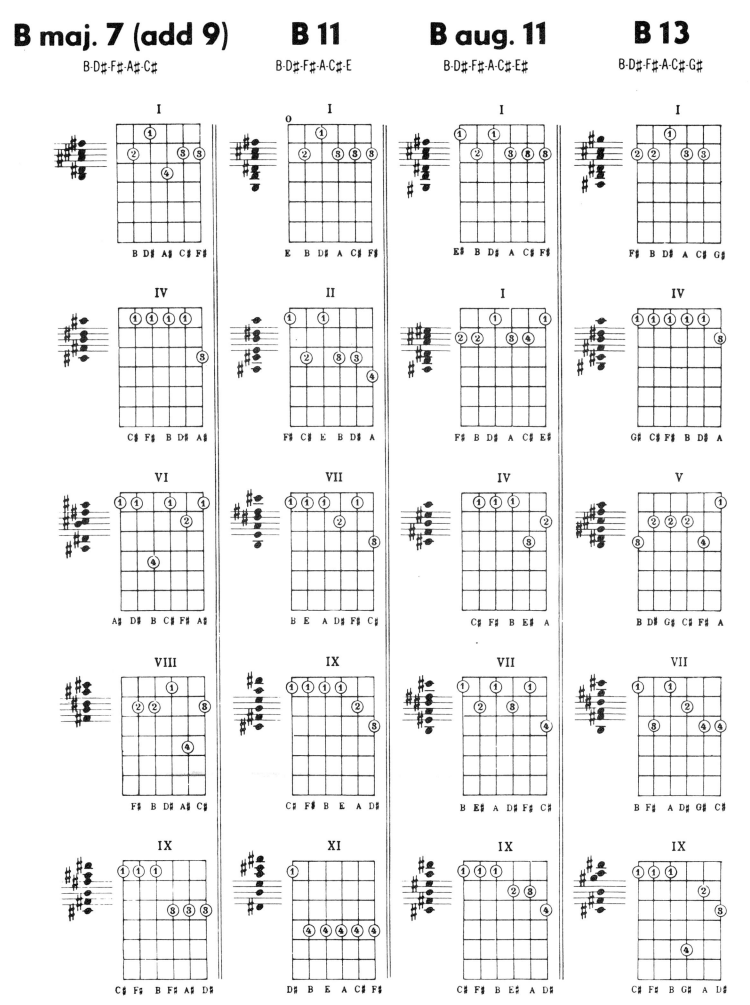